The H²Ed Guidebook

A Sourcebook of Inspiration & Practical Application

Created by: Marcella Runell & Martha Diaz

Foreword by: David Kirkland, Ph.D.

Edited by: Tatiana Forero Roy

Artwork by: Chris Soria

Published by the Hip-Hop Association Inc.

P.O Box 1181, New York, NY 10035

Copyright © 2007

ISBN: 978-0-6151-4262-3

Contents

Part I: Framing the Issues

Part II: Lessons

I.   Literacy and English Language Arts

II.   History, Global Studies and Geography

Charan Morris

III.   Music, Mathematics and Science

VI.   Social Justice, Tolerance and Diversity

Introduction

Peace and Blessings:

It is with much pleasure and honor that I present to you, the Hip-Hop Association's first Hip-Hop Education [H^{2}Ed] Guidebook (Volume I).

Since the inception of the H^{2}Ed Initiative, it has been a primary goal to create tools for our educators and youth. As a former New York City teacher, I know how important it is to have resources and support when you are a new teacher, especially if you're migrating from another city. Even if you're an experienced teacher, in order to achieve continuous success in the classroom, your lessons must stay relevant to today's world. We found out through our H^{2}Ed Summits that this was something that other educators needed and wanted.

In the pursuit of our mission, we realized that there were many educators and community activist using Hip-Hop culture as a learning tool to engage the youth. Although there had been discussions and conferences that have explored Hip-Hop in academia, there wasn't a consistent platform connecting, evaluating and validating their work. This cultural practice has been in existence since the genesis of Hip-Hop but now members of the Hip-Hop generation have infused in the United States education system; Hip-Hop Masters and those influenced by Hip-Hop culture are passing down their knowledge and keeping the spiritual legacy alive.

Hip-Hop Education is used in K-12 grade classrooms, after-school programs, prisons, community organizing, leadership camps, and universities. We have our own Hip-Hop doctrines, textbooks, children's books, nursery rhymes, dictionaries, documentaries, and even our own Hip-Hop Education Wiki; this phenomenon spans the globe. Countries such as Canada, France, Brazil, the Netherlands, and South Africa have embraced it, supported and continue to fund it. This is a movement and those dedicated to it want education reform to happen now. Our schools are inadequate and the system is faulty and unacceptable.

Hip-Hop is now 32 years old. It is inevitable that we would come to a keen awareness that makes sense of our existence. To many, Hip-Hop is a calling and way of life. To others, Hip-Hop is an

opportunity to create social change. Either way, our ancestors have provided us with a chance to utilize it to transform our lives.

I hope this guidebook helps you see Hip-Hop culture in a new light and gives you a glimpse of the myriad ways it can be used to empower our youth and community. The adept and accomplished authors in this guidebook graciously share with you their experiences and education models. They have generously donated their time and wisdom to our project. I want to thank all of them, the H^{2}A Advisors, H^{2}Ed Staff and Committee. Marcella thanks for making it happen.

Always Elevating Hip-Hop,

M:D

Founder and President

Hip-Hop Association

"Never doubt that a small group of thoughtful, committed people can change the world: indeed, it's the only thing that ever has." *Margaret Mead*

Foreword

From the moment Hip Hop met the classroom, the linguistic, pedagogical, and political struggle for justice in America education became clearer. No longer could American educators afford to disentangle social justice from American education. Hip Hop was revealing, all too well, our society's most heinous atrocities, even putting our classrooms on trial. From Nas's "Stillmatic" to Lauren Hill's "Miseducation," Hip Hop was teaching us that we needed to "start making some changes." And even when our classrooms were not changing, our students were. Like Hip Hop, they were evolving, lyrically revising their identities, interests, and ideas to meet the challenges of the new century. The authors in this guidebook have taken notice, boldly asserting that Hip Hop has a place in new century classrooms. Perhaps more importantly, they demonstrate how Hip Hop can inform all aspects of educational practice, especially in the interests of new century youth who find themselves equally struggling for social, cultural, and economic justice.

Bringing Hip Hop to class is a tough task. Therefore, this guidebook for educators is of immense importance because the messages delivered in classrooms are among those most valued in society. They have the potential for great impact on students' future lives, and we expect that seeds sown today will provide for a great harvest tomorrow. However, even though it seems quite reasonable to conclude that a message without a recipient is useless, a message without importance for its recipient is ignored. Too often in education we fail to keep these observations in mind. Of course, there are countless ways to help students feel like they genuinely belong in school, that they can benefit from education on a personal level and use it to interpret their environments on a daily basis. The use of Hip Hop to educate is one that appears particularly promising.

In order for the promises of Hip Hop to be realized, however, students must be given critical perspectives on messages received and processed. Such a perspective will enable students to distinguish between what aspects of incoming messages should and should not be valued, a capacity which is crucial to fruitful negotiation of everything from viewing magazine advertisements to reading news stories to listening to Hip Hop music. If those involved with the delivery of education maintain that rap and its relatives must stay out of the classroom because of concerns that these genres are gang-related, misogynistic, violent, materialistic, or simply badly written (Alexander-Smith, 2004), then we are in essence setting children free to parse out these musical messages entirely on their own. If, on the other hand, we invite Hip Hop into the classroom, not only might we have increased student interest and willingness, we might also provide opportunities for students to become appreciative and thoughtful consumers, capable of changing the world around them.

However, few educators could have predicted the influence that Hip Hop would have in education when it first hit the streets over three decades ago. Notwithstanding, Hip Hop education (or H^2Ed as it is referred to here) has, today, visibly emerged as the pedagogical discourse of new century youth (Morrell, 2002). Even in the phrase "it's hard out here for a pimp," Hip Hop's narrative of oppression articulates for youth a brazen critique of multiple iterations of social inequity still alive in the American capitalist economy. For the authors of this guidebook, Hip Hop provides more than a critique of society, but a pathway toward justice. For them the marginal have gained centrality in Hip Hop, and the vagaries of urban American social oppression have gained clarity and critique. Through this book, Hip Hop is used as a conduit, capable of transporting the social worlds and the social criticisms of disparate groups to the classroom core—to the once exclusive, once exalted, and once segregated world of "high" culture (see Dolby, 2003) masked as "high" literature, "high" art, and "high" education.

In breaking down the barriers between "high" and "low" literature, art and education, the new found validity of Hip Hop in this book raises serious questions about what counts as education in new century classrooms. Further, given its embedded criticism of social injustice, H^2Ed offers a range of critical perspectives (and possibilities) more transformative and more culturally grounded than many of the ones we currently embrace. As a result, what we teach and what students learn in our classrooms can never be the same. That is, Hip Hop has invited the world to change, but teaching Hip Hop for social justice invites teachers and students to change as well in our ongoing effort to manufacture more hopeful and more possible ways to exist.

David E. Kirkland, Ph.D.
Department of Teaching and Learning
New York University

12

References

Alexander-Smith, A. C. (2004). Feeling the rhythm of the critically conscious mind. *English Journal, 93*(3), 58-63.

1. Dolby, N. (2003). Popular culture and democratic practice. *Harvard Educational Review, 73*(3), 258-285.

Morrell, E., & Duncan-Andrade, J. M. R. (2002). Promoting academic literacy with urban youth through engaging hip-hop culture. *English Journal, 91*, 88-92.

About H²Ed

Formed in 2003 to serve educators and those committed to reaching youth through Hip-Hop culture, H²Ed was founded under the premise that Hip-Hop, the most influential cultural force today, has the power to educate, inform and empower today's youth.

By using a creative mix of standard educational formats and the popularity of Hip-Hop, we are committed to organizing the community we call T.O.P.S.Y. Partnership (Teachers, Organizations, Parents, Social Workers and Youth) to create a centralized repository for educational data, communication, and reform initiatives.

Why is H²Ed Necessary?

With public education in a state of crisis there is a growing need for innovation in the classroom. Current education models and respective curriculum tools are not effectively and equitably reaching children from all socio-economic classes. Learning is more effective when mediated through popular socio-cultural tools with which students identify. Educators have proven the success of mediated learning through critical pedagogical use of popular culture on a small-scale level. Hip-Hop is the accepted communication tool and primary umbrella of mainstream youth popular culture worldwide. The enduring quality, accessibility, rich history, and universal acceptance of Hip-Hop culture among youth renders it as a powerful pedagogical curriculum tool across subject areas for educators to utilize.

H²Ed GOALS

To inform all education and direct youth practitioners, and educational institutions of the applications of Hip-Hop culture as a tool to engage youth in academic and life skills
To reform pedagogical methods with new, engaging, youth based, and culturally relevant learning tools. To present and advocate Hip-Hop culture as an academic discipline and art form that can be used as a vehicle to create community building, academic engagement, inter-generational relationships, and future leaders

Our Assumptions about Hip-Hop Education:

It is a layered approach founded on social justice education, embedded in hip-hop culture, relying on critical pedagogy and community activism to teach hip-hop as subject, hip-hop as pedagogy to teach another subject, and/or hip-hop as the warm-up hook or bridge to draw students into the class.

- It is not the answer to urban education problems, white supremacy, or other societal ills. It can be a tool for liberation when utilized in an affirming and exploratory way.

- It doesn't require or encourage educators to speak in Ebonics, slang or learn how to rap, dance, dress in a particular way, or otherwise appropriate a culture that is not their own.

- It does require you to merge your knowledge as a teacher with the knowledge of the students; creating a learning environment that is mutually beneficial.

- Social identities matter for both the teacher and the student. We all have a worldview that is informed by experiences within our various communities; it is not helpful to ignore this in the classroom.

- It requires that you have an understanding and belief that levels and types of oppression exist; such as institutional and cultural racism, classism, sexism, etc. and Hip-Hop both perpetuates and interrogates these ISMs. It does not exist in a vacuum. Hip-Hop was started by and for young people of color in urban areas; this should never be left out of the analysis, discussion or history-otherwise it is likely to replicate oppression.

- It is essential to your understanding as an educator that you respect and believe in Hip-Hop as a culture complete with agreed upon elements, as well as shared language, dress, style, history, values and unifying capabilities.

- Geography matters. Hip-Hop culture generally has local influences, heroes, stories, and values. Hip-Hop music in Israel will likely sound very different than Hip-Hop music in Atlanta, Georgia. Utilize your students' expertise to investigate how the narratives and culture are influenced by geographic locations.

- Hip-Hop has a short shelf life particularly with young people; as soon as you figure it out as a teacher, it has probably become dated. Accepting the short shelf life and the desire for youth culture to be counter-culture will serve you well. It is ok not to know what is "hot." It is more important that you are open to learning how to keep the students engaged.

Utilizing Hip-Hop music and culture to reach students is based on tenets of critical pedagogy and Popular education theories and practices. The methodology is transferable beyond Hip-Hop culture.

About the H²Ed Guidebook

This Guidebook was conceived as part of the Hip-Hop Association's Education initiative (H²Ed). The lessons are standards-referenced, and unique in their approach to traditional academic disciplines, as well as informal educational settings. The lessons are all actual lesson plans that have been successfully used across the United States and Canada. Some of the lessons contain considerable background information on the artists or subject matter, while other lessons are more general. A few of the lessons contain explicit language, but in an effort to honor the creativity of the authors and authenticity of the music as art, the content was not edited for explicit language. The age levels vary from 5th-12th grades. The position papers are meant to frame the issues from various perspectives including scholarly research and practical application.

The mission of H²Ed (www.h2ed.net.) is to serve as a resource for educators and those committed to helping children succeed in school by using the power of hip-hop culture as a learning tool. This is achieved by compiling and maintaining a comprehensive list of educational resources, products and services available for our educators; as well as by providing important networking opportunities, and by advocating on both the institutional and grassroots levels for educational reform.

The H²Ed Guidebook offers the opportunity to see the different ways in which Hip-Hop can be used as an educational tool. This is only the beginning of your journey with H²Ed. You must educate yourself and continue to study and appreciate the evolution of Hip-Hop Education.

Acknowledgements

This guidebook is truly a labor of love. Every single lesson plan and position paper was generously submitted at no cost to the organization. Educators from all over the United States and Canada including Los Angeles, Oakland, Seattle, Atlanta, Chicago, Toronto and New York City submitted their lesson plans, syllabi, essays and suggestions for how to make the guidebook more user-friendly. I believe this book to be especially useful because it was written by teachers, not curriculum developers or scholars, for teachers. These lessons have all been used effectively with students in various contexts and settings.

It is my hope that these lessons and position papers will activate your imagination, help you to feel connected to a bigger movement, encourage you to try something new in your school or community; and that you feel that we are positively representing Hip-Hop culture and the Hip-Hop generation.

On behalf of the Hip-Hop Association, we'd also like to give a big shout out to our Hip-Hop forefathers who have made this book possible today: Kool Herc, Afrika Bambaataa, and Grandmaster Flash. We'd also like to thank Rolando Brown, Chris Soria and One9. Also, we'd like to give another shout out to the hundreds of educators and organizations that use Hip-Hop as an educational instrument. They join the likes of Dr. Cornell West, Dr. Tricia Rose, Toni Blackman, Danny Hoch, Jeff Chang, Cashus D, Dr. Gwendolyn Pough, Marcell Diallo, Rha Goddess, Carlos McBride, Adisa Banjoka, Baba, Kamilah Forbes, April Silver, Byron Hurt (Beyond Beats and Rhymes), Amaris Mesa, Dr. Michael Eric Dyson, Paul Flores, Ken Swift, Jeff Duncan-Andrades, Dr. David Stovall, Daphne Farganis, Safahri Rha, Toofly, Dr. Thandi Hicks-Harper, Marinieves Alba, Bryonn Bain, Dr. James White, Michael Cirelli, Priya Parmar, Shirley Steinberg, Joe Kincheloe, K Swift, Ora Wise, Universal Zulu Nation, Hip-Hop Congress, Hip Hop LEADS, Temple of Hip-Hop, Kuumba Academy, El Puente Academy, Guerrilla Arts, The Center for Black Literature, Medgar Ever's College, Sistaz of the Underground, Urban Word NYC, Full Circle, Blackout Arts Collective, Edutainment, TATS Cru, Word, Beats and Life, Weapon of Mass Expression…

Special thanks to all the teachers, editors, workshop participants, students, community members, scholars, partners, and friends who offered suggestions and feedback for creating a user-friendly, self-published, community-based resource. A special thank you to Tatiana Forero Puerta for your support and assistance in organizing and editing this book, and to Martha Diaz for bringing me on board as part of the Hip-Hop Association's H^{2}Ed initiative to make this dream a reality. And a special, heartfelt thank you to David Hall aka DJ Trends, my partner, friend and colleague who constantly reminds me why I still love Hip-Hop; and why this work, when done with integrity, is so very important to our community.

Marcella Runell

Director of Education, H^{2}Ed Initiative
Hip-Hop Association

PART I: FRAMING THE ISSUES

Keisha Green, M.A., Doctoral Student

Blackout Arts Collective & Emory University, Atlanta, GA

Check It: Reflections on Hip-Hop & Education

Jade Caines, M. Ed, Doctoral Student

Emory University, Atlanta, GA

It's All About the Benjamins: The Marriage Between Hip Hop, Adolescence, and Consumerism

Nicole Duncan-Smith, Parent, Children's Author "I AM Hip Hop"

From Sesame Street to Beat Street to Your Street

David Stovall, Ph.D., Assistant Professor, Policy Studies and African-American Studies

University of Illinois at Chicago

Hip-Hop and Social Studies for Critical Analysis

Marcella Runell, M.Ed., Doctoral Candidate

University of Massachusetts, Amherst

The Organic Connection Between Hip-Hop and Social Justice Education: A Theoretical Model for Activism

Kenji Jasper, Author, Columnist, Educator

Brooklyn, New York

The Lesson 2.0

Keisha Green, M.A.

Doctoral Student

Emory University, Atlanta, GA

Check It: Reflections on Hip-Hop & Education

"When they beat us in the heads with them books, it don't reach us."

--Dead Prez *They Schools*

Check it. Whether or not you agree with using Hip Hop in the classroom, an indisputable fact remains: The lyrics from the popular track *They Schools* by Hip Hop duo Dead Prez capture the sentiment of many youth, particularly youth from historically marginalized communities across the country. Today, public schools in the United States scramble to prepare students for standardized high stakes tests using scripted curriculum, voluminous textbooks, or canonized literature—all of which include content that is rarely reflective of or accessible to the student body they serve. Based on my classroom experiences as an African American student and teacher, I am convinced that culturally responsive teaching and learning practices significantly enhance student academic achievement and overall engagement, particularly among black and brown students. Regarding twenty-first century urban public school classroom instruction, what is more culturally responsive than Hip Hop?

Once upon a time, not long ago…I was an English Instructor for a mixed group of ninth and tenth grade students who were participants in the Talent Search Academic Academy at Columbia University's Double Discover Center, a high school summer enrichment program in New York City. I wanted to construct a dynamic space for students to learn and create together. And, because it was summertime, I aimed to liberate the traditional educational experience from its usual structure, while still maintaining a rigorous environment where students were challenged to think, read, and write critically. My students and I accomplished all of the above goals using Hip-Hop music and culture to explore our class topic: *Challenging notions of the American dream.* Serendipitously, that same year, Sean Combs a.k.a. P. Diddy starred in the revival of the acclaimed play, *A Raisin in the Sun*, which was to be one of our

main texts for the course. What incredible synergy. Together, my students and I critically analyzed the social, cultural, political, and historical context of Lorraine Hansberry's award-winning play about a black family living on the Southside of Chicago during the 1950's. This story of hope, despite the despair of deferred dreams, mirrors the origins of Hip-Hop. Throughout the four weeks, students compared "Harlem" by Langston Hughes to Hip-Hop verses with similar meanings, and connected the plot details and conflicts evident in the play with current events and present day struggles as expressed through Hip-Hop music. During a character analysis activity, the class selected Hip-Hop lyrics to illustrate the traits, attitudes, feelings, and aspirations of each character in the play. Finally, students produced a contemporary Hip-Hop soundtrack to accompany their dramatic presentation of an excerpt of *A Raisin in the Sun*, but not without having to provide evidence to support why each song was appropriate for the story.

For my students, Hip-Hop was the bridge between their lived experiences, prior knowledge, and academic literacy. Through Hip-Hop, I taught the New York State learning standards for high school English Language Arts. Students successfully demonstrated their ability to draw conclusions, make inferences, identify stylistic elements and literacy devices, paraphrase, and clearly express ideas in writing. That summer, I did not use an English Language Arts or literature textbook. Instead, I used a primary source, a text written by an African American woman spliced with jazz and blues. Lorraine Hansberry's drama *A Raisin in the Sun* is the soundtrack of an American experience—much like Hip-Hop is the soundtrack for many urban students. Hip-Hop hooked my students who, as a result, willingly participated in classroom discussions and responded to the readings through essays that were written passionately and skillfully. That summer, I took a risk and tried something new, believing that my students would benefit. I did not have to know or even like all of the Hip-Hop music that my students listened to with regularity. However, I was committed to learning more about the beats and rhymes that narrate their lives. I made my students' voices and interests central to the educational experience. Now, it's your turn to rock the mic.

21

H²Ed

Nicole Duncan-Smith

Parent, Children's Author "I AM Hip Hop"

From Sesame Street to Beat Street to Your Street

Bridging the gap is cliché. As parents, we know that children don't speak our language and they know that we don't speak theirs. America as a whole recognizes the need for cross-generational communication. But that need is hidden beneath all the other "isms" that plague our society. Patriotic and Terrorist dogma headline the dailies of our minds. Racism in education, the workforce and in the media surely tugs at the hearts of old civil rights champions who have long lost their strides and even feminism and homosexuality gets the attention of the politicians in a fashion that we thought would be obsolete by this millennium. There is always a cause to champion that is more urgent than catering to our children (specifically poor Black and Latino children). After all, we feed them, clothe them and we give a firm economy to forge their livelihood. And though, we can blame it on the fast-paced world we live in or the epidemic of drugs that steamrolled an entire generation in the eighties, we have to yield to something being lost in translation between kids and their parents. Hip-Hop has a bona-fide solution for change. It can be used as the translator. Hip-Hop can be used as an interpreter to get our very useful life lessons to the open and sponge-like minds of our children.

Music and culture have always been used to teach children how to function in social and academic environments. You will not find one toddler who does not know the "Alphabet song". With that one little ditty more children have learned the English language than by site recognition of the words. How does one take that kind of potential catalyst and create a classroom that invigorates students? How do you inspire them to dream larger than the realities outside their windows? And once they do begin to aspire to greatness intellectually and socially, rather than financially, how do you bridge the gap in community so that these questions can be answered. Rap music, the 3rd element of Hip-Hop, is key to embarking in such an exercise.

In my lecture from Sesame Street to Beat Street to Your Street, we examine the ways that have worked in the past for students. We then work from that model and includes aspects of popular culture-Hip-Hop in particular and find relationships between the lesson plans and the very block that the child lives on. A simple example is using rap lyrics to translate difficult

22

historical fiction such as Shakespeare or Chaucer- or for parents seeking to engage their children in conversation, create a family project that allows for role play and the usage of a self made glossary to learn exactly what in the world they are saying. You may laugh but it is necessary, because the lingo changes daily. As a whole community the use of technology can allow a glimpse of the global perspective that Hip-Hop has always had.

Don't be shocked! Hip-Hop was developed in the South Bronx by former gang members who were so enlightened by change in the midst of tragedy-they created Unity jams that promoted parties and used skills and intellect to settle street beefs. Their theories weren't Freudian but age-old lessons like "The World Is Bigger Than Our Block" and "There Is Nothing To Outrageous for Someone Who Believes" and "We Deserve Better Because We Are Human". You might not know that because you don't speak their language. And they might now know we all want the same things because the language barrier is that... a barrier. Thus creating a larger wedge between the generations. Hip-Hop is not the enemy. Not in the classroom. Not in the kitchen and not in the boardroom. It is a cultural expression (point blank) and we have to access that like Braille for a blind person, in order to access the universe of our children.

Jade Caines, M. Ed

Doctoral Candidate

Emory University, Atlanta, GA

It's All About the Benjamins: The Marriage Between Hip Hop, Adolescence, and Consumerism

Music has always been an integral part of American culture, especially youth culture. Consider the swing era of the 1920s, the bebop era of the 1950s, and the rock 'n' roll era of the 1960s. Youth rebellion has generally been linked to the tunes being played and the songs being sung.

The development of the radio in the 1920s came at just the right time for teenagers. Not only did songs express the angst they were feeling, but it allowed them to share those feelings with millions of other kids across the country. Youth, as a subculture, was intricately linked to the rise of media and popular music. Adolescents have similar experiences; they pass through peer groups and use music as a badge, a means of identifying and articulating emotion. Therefore, music functions within youth subculture as a way of defining the self, creating collective excitement, and bringing about a sense of solidarity and subcultural consciousness (Epstein, 1994).

School helped to define youth culture by physically segregating teens so that they spent the majority of their day in a world dominated by peers; similarly, mass media ideologically segregated kids. Youthful language, style of dress, values, goals, behavior, and especially music became increasingly foreign to adults (Wartella & Mazzarella, 1990). This opened the door for the music industry to directly target adolescents for product consumption, thereby molding a separate pre-teen/teen culture. Adolescents erected walls around *their* fashion, *their* language, and *their* music, creating a distinct consumer market.

Therefore, it is no surprise that hip hop, since the late 1970s, has dominated most of the adolescent consumer market. The term *rap music* (including party rap, socially conscious rap, gangsta rap, and commercial rap) is often used synonymously with the term hip hop; this, however, is erroneous. Although hip hop can be referred to as a musical genre, it is much more than that. It represents a culture that spans far beyond just beats and lyrics; it includes films, publications, fashion, language, political activism etc. This chapter deals with the convergence

of hip hop, consumerism, and adolescence. More specifically, it will answer the following question: How has the commercialization of hip hop lead to corporate exploitation of the adolescent, hip hop generation?

Big Spenders: The Youth Consumer Market

Adolescence, the period covering ages 12 to 18, is an important time in the socialization of youth. It is a period of rapid change in psychological, social, and emotional development; it is also a time when youth orient themselves towards consumerist behavior patterns. During adolescence, the relatively dependent child is transformed into the relatively autonomous young consumer (Gunter & Furnham, 1998). They develop consumption-related skills and quickly become savvy customers.

Several factors influence this shift. First, adolescent's expenditures and discretionary income increase during this child development phase. Either parents increase allowance or adolescents acquire part-time employment; whatever the means, they simply have more money to spend and more things they *have* to get.

Second, they begin to develop "product preferences" which sometimes continue well into their adult years. A study of brand loyalty done for *Seventeen* magazine found that a high percentage of adult women used the same brands from their teenage years (Gunter & Furnham, 1998). This indicates to market researchers that the youth consumer market can be an extremely profitable demographic.

Last, their need for independence from family, coupled with their need for peer acceptance, means that marketers can advertise directly to the adolescent, instead of to parents. Until adolescence, children had to nag their parents in order to acquire desired commodities. They did not start receiving an allowance until teen years and, even then, only 33 percent of the youngest teens receive a regular, structured stipend (Zollo, 2004). Therefore, if children and young teens wanted to purchase commodities, mom and dad had to approve. Once they turn 16, however, it seems that teens have more control over their finances and do not have to justify every purchase to their parents. More than 50 percent of teenagers age 16 or older work part-time jobs (compared to 11 percent under age 16). Therefore, they are more self-reliant and able to exercise autonomy in purchasing decisions.

Pimping a culture: Marketing and Hip Hop Consumerism

It is easy to say that hip hop fans are the biggest spenders (Twitchell, 1999). Especially since inner-city styles and cultural practices steeped in the hip hop tradition have been such a dominant influence on, and definer of, popular culture (Schor, 2004). Marketers have capitalized from (and some may even say created) the hip hop consumer market.

Advertising is a billion dollar industry that uses anything to sell products. Music is one medium that, for a long time now, has been a great selling instrument. Research indicates that music actually ties with humor as the most important element in pre-teen/adolescent commercials (Siegel, Coffey, & Livingston, 2001). Therefore, marketers have developed specific strategies in targeting the adolescent consumer.

One strategy, which has been used for decades, is a propaganda technique called testimonial. Television and radio commercials, magazine advertisements, and billboard ads feature famous people (many of them hip hop artists) to promote a given product. Teens eagerly mimic the styles they see on their favorite musical performers (Zollo, 2004). Beyonce has sold Pepsi, Busta Rhymes has sold Mountain Dew, and KRS-One has sold Sprite. There are multitudes of hip hop artists that endorse a variety of products (not just soft drinks). Marketers hope that associating their product with someone famous (read influential) will increase sales. For a long time, this strategy has been extremely profitable.

Since the 1980s, companies have been giving free commodities to rappers who then wear them in music videos, thus starting the new urban trend (Schor, 2004). This strategy, known as buzz marketing, is cheap and delivers good bang for the buck. It is not limited to simple product placement, either; it can include distribution of hip hop CDs at urban clubs and adolescent parties, the use of e-mail lists to advertise products, and peer to peer marketing (where young kids are recruited to use their friendship networks in order to create a "buzz" around a certain product). Buzz marketing is part of why promotions seem to be almost everywhere we turn.

Another marketing ploy includes a strategy called "under-the-radar". Many teen marketers have discovered that most adolescents are cynical towards advertising and tired of being manipulated. One pre-teen in a focus group commented "Don't you know, you can't have an ad saying (or implying) 'buy me, buy me, buy me.' It has to be cool and fun. If we like your ad, then we'll like your product (Seigel, Coffey, & Livingston, 2001). Advertisers have taken

note and develop advertising campaigns that are subtle and fall under the radar of teenage cynicism. Some companies pay deejays to put their theme songs into music mixes (Schor, 2004). This practice, called deejay promotion, is usually featured on radio stations and is extremely successful. It is generally hard to identify these advertisements because they closely resemble hip hop songs. Skillfully camouflaged, pre-teens (and possibly even teenagers) listening to the radio may think the Mountain Dew spot is a new hip hop song.

Other teen marketing firms have used the Internet to push under the radar marketing schemes. They pay representatives to infiltrate chat rooms, posing as teenagers, in order to learn about popular trends and promote specific brands. These representatives do not have to be teenagers, as the medium allows visual anonymity. Cornerstone, a New York-based teen marketing firm, however, has admitted to hiring teenagers to log onto chat rooms where they pose as just another fan of one of Cornerstone's clients.

Last, some marketers have tried reverse psychology on adolescent consumers by releasing anti-marketing campaigns. Sprite, for example, put out ads in the early 90s that poked fun at advertising. They featured famous celebrities that said *not* to listen to celebrities. Some teens may have bought into this new "anti-marketing" marketing strategy, but others saw through the hoax; they knew that Sprite was trying to portray themselves as cool in order to win credibility with media-savvy teens.

Sprite, however, did eventually capitalize from the under-the-radar marketing ploys. Marketing executives for Sprite realized that they should do less marketing of their product and more marketing of their understanding of hip hop lifestyle. They featured hip hop artists performing while holding a Sprite can; they financially supported concerts that displayed Sprite propaganda; they partnered with popular television stations to subversively promote their product. In the end, Sprite's new tactics worked. The soft drink is now an icon in the hip hop world. They successfully married a corporation to a culture.

Cool hunting

Marketers are aware of the fact that most kids want to be a part of a culture that represents *coolness*. It is *cool* to be associated with being older than one's age; it is *cool* to live life dangerously; it is *cool* to rebel against the status quo and adult hegemony. This desire to be cool is a phenomenon in adolescent culture and has led many teen marketing firms to hunt for

the definition of *cool*.

Adolescent market researchers spend tremendous amounts of time searching for those kids that represent cool. They say that 20 percent of adolescents are trendsetters (also known as early adopters), while the other 80 percent are followers. They send out correspondents/culture spies to look for those kids who are forward in their thinking and leaders in their peer groups.

Dee Dee Gordon and Sharon Lee started a company called *Look Look* that specializes in adolescent market research. Only 30 years old, Gordon is considered to be one of the best in the teen market research field. She charges high fees as a consultant to companies interested in targeting the youth demographic; for $20,000 each, companies are granted access to the *Look Look* website in order to gain insight into what's hot and what's not in teen culture.

Many other teen market research firms conduct focus groups. They pay teenagers nominal fees to identify their opinions on "coolness". These focus groups are supposed to reveal the most successful and popular advertising strategies targeting these cool adolescents. Marketing firms value the opinions of focus group participants and use them in developing effective advertising strategies that target cool youth.

Once advertisers tapped into adolescent culture, they quickly learned that urban, Black youth were the ultimate definers of cool. A Philadelphia-based market research firm called *MEE* (Motivational, Educational Entertainment) Productions put out a study in 1992 that showed how Black urban youth have long been trendsetters for what's cool (Kitwana, 2005). *The MEE Report: Reaching the Hip Hop Generation* was their first major breakthrough study and it was followed by another report called *The National Lifestyle Survey of African American Inner City Youth*. Both studies showed that Black adolescents set the bar for what's cool in popular adolescent culture.

The notion of coolness also permeates the successful marriage of hip hop and consumerism. Part of being cool is having something that others do not (Schor, 2004). It makes adolescents feel special and sparks that drive to find the next cool item. Marketers convey the idea that wealth is cool. Material excess, having lots of money, career achievement, and a lifestyle to go with it are all highly valued in the marketing world's definition of what's hot and what's not. Living modestly means living like a loser.

The connection to inner-city life may sound like a contradiction to the idea that cool is

exclusive and upscale, but it is resolved by the fact that many hip hop artists are wealthy and conspicuous consumers. Soft drink manufacturers, candy corporations, and apparel companies target segments of the adolescent population by placing kids that are slightly older than the target group in advertisements. Coolness, also associated with edginess, is about the taboo and forbidden, and has taken root in advertisements that consist of hip hop elements.

The commodification of the hip hop lifestyle is deeply embedded in this notion of coolness. "Street culture has proven to be a potent commodity because its aesthetic offers an authentic threatening edginess that is very attractive both to White suburban kids…and to urban cultural elites… We now have the commodification of a virulent, dangerous 'other' lifestyle…. Gangsta." Incorporating this "gangsta" lifestyle in advertising campaigns has been extremely lucrative for companies targeting the adolescent consumer market. Commodifiable assets are now things that have always had negative images attached— the urban neighborhood, the pain of being poor, and the alienation experienced by black kids. Through hip hop music, the most negative projections of African Americans became the most popular for young people (Chuck D, 1997). It is cool to be on the side of the criminal. The consumer giants are benefiting from this increasing acceptance of rebelliousness.

50 Cent, a popular hip hop artist, embodies this cool, gangsta image that marketers use to target the trendsetters. An article in *Teen People* featured music artists of the year and one adolescent commented "I'm more of a rock guy, but I listen to whatever 50 Cent puts out… it's brilliant to see him [feud with other rappers]— it seems like whenever someone starts an argument with him, 50 wins! He's really cool… 50 doesn't just talk the talk. A lot of rappers do that without the scars to prove it, but 50's as real as it gets ("Artists of the Year," 2005, December/January)." This adolescent, as well as many others around the country, admire rapper 50 Cent's "real" street credentials and calls it cool. He has been shot nine times and is notorious for his ongoing feud with rapper Ja Rule. In one song he stated, "That kid is a fraud…. [He] grew up a Jehovah's Witness. While we were selling crack, he was knocking on people's doors every Saturday." ("Top 10 Celeb Disses," 2005, September). A trendsetter would easily identify 50 cents lyrics as cool. Unfortunately, in this example, religious commitment can make someone appear fraudulent, while selling drugs is glamorized. Many adolescents glorify rappers (like 50 Cent) because of, and not in spite of, their gangsta lifestyle.

The commodification of gangsta life has been extremely lucrative for many hip hop artists, including 50 Cent. For example, he has gained much financial success through his albums; his debut album *Get Rich or Die Tryin'* broke records by selling over 12 million units worldwide, while his sophomore album sold so many copies that he became the first artist to have four songs in the top ten of Billboard's Hot 100 since The Beatles in 1964 (50 Cent, 2005). His albums, however, are just the beginning of his lucrative career. 50 Cent's business empires include: a record label (G-Unit Records, a division of Interscope Records), apparel/footwear ventures (G-Unit clothing and footwear and joint ventures through the Ecko clothing company and Reebok), vitamin water (Formula 50, through Glacéau's Vitamin Water), a watch line (G-Unit Watches, through Jacob & Co.), and a video game (50 Cent: Bulletproof, through Vivendi Games). His book *From Pieces to Weight* rounds out his cool, gangsta image. It is apparent that 50 Cent epitomizes the cool rapper that marketers use to sell their products.

It is easy for adolescents to idolize the hip hop lifestyle that consists of fame and glory. Unfortunately, many adolescents do not understand the perils of the gangsta life. Take, for example, the life of Notorious B.I.G. His album is an example of a hustler's life journey turned tragic:

We boarded with the story of his birth, strategically stopped to view his dysfunctional, warring family, his first robbery, his first stint in jail, murder, drug-dealing, getting paid, partying, sexin', rappin, mayhem, and death. Biggie's player persona might have momentarily convinced the listener that he was livin' phat without a care in the world but other moments divulged his inner hell. The chorus of "Everyday Struggle": *I don't wanna live no more / Sometimes I see death knockin' at my front door* reveals that "Big Poppa" was also plagued with guilt, regret, and depression. The album ultimately ended with his [death] (Morgan, 1999).

This is just one rapper, but he represents many other rap artists in the hip hop community. What often passes as "a 40 and a blunt" good times in most hip hop songs is really alcoholism and substance abuse. When African American males can talk so cavalierly about killing each other and then reveal that they have no expectation to see their twenty-first birthday, that is depression masquerading as machismo. It is obvious that the consumerist lifestyle, which is underridden by the gangsta lifestyle, is anything but glamorous. Unfortunately, most adolescents think being a gangsta is cool and marketers simply profit from the masked pain of hip hop artists.

The Lighter Side: White kids and Hip Hop

Bakari Kitwana, author of *Why White Kids Love Hip Hop* describes three concentric circles of White kids who consume hip hop music. The center circle consists of White kids who consider themselves rappers (also known as hip hop practitioners). The second outer circle, which can overlap with the first, includes White kids who are deeply immersed within hip hop culture and Black youth culture; they understand hip hop as an extension of Black culture. These White adolescents are at ease with Blacks and do not consider the race a novelty. The third and largest ring consists of kids who love hip hop simply because it is a part of dominant youth culture; they have no allegiance to the genre and are what Kitwana terms *free-floating fans* (Kitwana, 2005).

Kitwana also describes three concentric circles of Black kids who love hip hop. The small, inner circle houses the stereotypical buppies who are detached from Black youth culture, but are occasional hip hop listeners. The second, slightly larger, circle is made up of those who consume hip hop because it is just another must-have commodity that is popular amongst adolescents. The third, and largest, circle consists of Black adolescents who live and breathe hip hop; these kids are true fans of the genre and are practitioners of the art form.

Research indicates that age trumps race and region as key factors in determining people's musical tastes and preferences (Quinn, 2005). Therefore, it is no surprise that adolescents of all ethnicities and cultural backgrounds love hip hop. This, however, is not a new discovery. From the nascent years of hip hop, White and Black adolescents had common experiences and feelings that several musical genres reflected. Billboard reported that the gangsta rap group N.W.A (Niggaz with Attitude) sold out in many rock/heavy metal outlets. The same themes— anger, rebellion, and apathy— appeared in both musical genres. Corporate entities do market research to determine how these parallel themes will yield the most profit. MTV, for example, used to program heavy metal shows (like *Headbanger's Ball*) and rap shows (like *Yo! MTV Raps*) in close time slots because the audience demographics remained constant throughout both.

This explains why Black Nationalist groups like Public Enemy had such a large, loyal, White fan base. They uniquely balanced rap danceability and rock aggression without alienating

Black or White adolescents (George, 1998). One could argue that their message, which rebelled against the status quo, served as a vehicle to unite adolescents across cultures. Offspring of the Public Enemy wave included N.W.A, Snoop Doggy Dog, and Tupac Shakur. Although the musical styles (and even sub-genres) vary, they all challenged authoritarianism and hegemony. Rap artists post-Public Enemy represented a new genre of rap called gangsta rap and teenagers, especially boys, embraced the message wholeheartedly.

Ain't Nuthin But a "G" Thang: Commodifying the Gangsta Lifestyle

A genre of rap music, gangsta rap graphically describes life on the streets of tough, Black, inner-city neighborhoods (Springhall, 1998). In order to make sense of the origins of gangsta rap it is important to understand its trajectory. First appearing in the mid-1980s and tapering off around the early 1990s, the genre was a direct by-product of the crack epidemic and all that occurred as a result of that era, including the widespread incarceration of African American men (George, 1998). A 1990 report stated that one in four African American males between twenty and twenty-nine—610,000 men in total— were either behind bars or on probation. This number was high because of the crack trade, the aggressive sentencing of low-level drug offenses, and a hopelessness that pervaded inner-city, African American communities. Major themes of gangsta rap include loyalty to your group of friends, adoption of a hardened mentality towards mainstream society, and hatred of authority. All of these themes were present in African American, inner-city communities. Gangsta rap reflected these feelings through a musical medium; one could call them reporters for the Black CNN.

The genre received much criticism, however, for its foul language, misogynistic lyrics about women, and celebration of violence. When gangsta rapper Ice-T released a song entitled *Cop Killer* (which explicitly spoke about killing police officers), the $16 billion entertainment giant Time Warner dropped the recording star (Springhall, 1998). They also relinquished their half of Interscope Records, the distributors of the hard-core Death Row label which featured strictly gangsta rappers. It was reported that Warner Bros. executives (a subsidiary of Time Warner) received death threats and that stockholders threatened to pull out of the company (http://en.wikipedia.org/wiki/Cop_Killer). The shift in support was also because of public outcry concerning the controversial song. *Cop Killer* was blamed for several police shootings and the

LA riots. Ice-T defended his song, stating that he was speaking in character and that freedom of speech gives him the right to express outrage at police brutality cases such as Rodney King and countless others.

Surprisingly, despite the criticism and negative attention, gangsta rap achieved commercial success. One of the earliest gangsta rap groups, N.W.A, sold over 900,000 copies of *Niggaz4Life* within the first week's release (Kitwana, 2005). Some of the original members include Dr. Dre, Eazy-E, and Ice Cube. Later on, Dr. Dre went solo and his album *The Chronic* went quadruple-platinum. He featured artist Snoop Doggy Dogg on the album, who also eventually branched out. His album, *Doggy Style*, went 5 times platinum (http://en.wikipedia.org/wiki/N.W.A.).

Record sales show that gangsta rap proved to be a powerful vehicle in reaching America's alienated, yet consumer-driven, youth. But although they may have been outraged at prison industrial policies, racially-motivated crimes, and poverty-stricken conditions, adolescents still spent money. It wasn't long before companies recognized the new, although young, market. Hence, the matrimonial union between rap and commercialism (which existed pre-gangsa rap) reached heightened levels of publicity.

The 40 ounce club

In the late 1980s, St. Ides was one of the first products to successfully link up with gangsta rap culture. In 1988, the manufacturer's that sell the alcohol brand called *St. Ides*, fired the Four Tops and hired rap artists to endorse their product. With a hip hop producer at the helm, rappers created their own St. Ides rap jingles. The product that received the most attention, the St. Ides' 40-ounce Olde English 800 (also referred to as a *40*) became an iconic symbol in the gangsta rap subculture. In the 80s, the marketing campaign focused on the poor and working-class urban identity, which conveniently overlapped with the angst-ridden youth culture. Thus the 40-ounce culture was born.

St. Ides' sales skyrocketed and it became a corporate leader in 1991—the same year that gangsta rap first topped the pop album charts in America. Simultaneously, gangsta rap and the 40-ounce club permeated popular film. *Boyz N the Hood*, starring gangsta rapper, turned producer, turned actor Ice Cube, had plentiful scenes that strategically placed St. Ides' 40-ounce bottle in frames.

There was some protest about the blatant marketing strategies that targeted youth in general, and black youth specifically. State officials described the St. Ides' ads as "illegal, false, and obscene" and called for a governmental crack down. There was even a complaint filed with the Bureau of Alcohol, Tobacco, and Firearms over St. Ides advertising. It stated that the ads glamorized gangs and often contained obscene and sexual references.

In the late 1980s St. Ides was one of the few national sponsors to use rap music in their marketing schemes. By 1991, gangsta rap, with the help of St. Ides, was generating more than $700 million in recording industry sales, about 10 percent of the market. It is evident that the marriage between hip hop, adolescence, and consumerism has existed for over two decades.

"I Want My MTV!": The Advent of Music Television

The evolution of hip hop has been affected by many things— drugs, violence, poverty, etc. Arguably, however, none has had more of an impact on hip hop than music videos. Without question, music videos have had an enormous impact on the commercialization of hip hop. "Through its images, the attitude and obsessions of urban America have been broadcast around the world, igniting fascination and fear, indignation and imitation, in the minds of youths [everywhere]" (George, 1998). Music videos, with the help of two television networks, have made hip hop culture accessible to all.

During the late 1980s, Music Television (widely known as *MTV*) and Black Entertainment Television (usually called *BET*) were most influential in advertising hip hop music through videos. Initially, however, MTV had a hands-off attitude toward all forms of Black music in its earlier years. Defining themselves as a televised rock radio station, Black music didn't make the cut. Even BET, which catered to the rotation of rhythm and blues (R&B), (surprisingly) did not embrace hip hop during most of the 1980s.

This new musical genre, however, was causing such a stir in the urban markets that both MTV and BET could no longer ignore its popularity. MTV eventually gave in and birthed its first hip hop show, *Yo, MTV Raps!*. It aired the latest hip hop music videos and urban fashion trends. Hip hop was no longer restricted to one market; it successfully reached the largest record-buying audience in the country, which increased record sales, thereby encouraging the development of more hip hop videos.

Similar to MTV, BET also tried to maintain its original focus, but the success of *Yo, MTV*

Raps! forced them to change directions. To compete, they launched *Rap City*, their own version of a hip hop-centered show. It is clear that these television programs were heavy corporate advertising mediums and had the potential to significantly impact hip hop consumerism. Not only did advertisers target the hip hop generation during commercial breaks, but hip hop music videos were instrumental in promoting the latest consumer trends.

The cycle went as follows: performers would latch on to a new clothing style from the streets (or get freebies from marketers using the under-the-radar marketing ploy), that style would be showcased in a video, and adolescent audiences would adopt that new style (George, 1998). An outfit worn in certain high-profile urban centers could quickly become a national, and sometimes international, trend due to the hip hop community and the power of television.

Currently, music videos are still influential vehicles for hip hop consumption. Shows like *Total Request Live* and *106 and Park* (both aired on MTV and BET, respectively) are cultural symbols in the teenage world. They are hour-long commercials that advertise everything from movies to footwear. Music is simply the backdrop; consumption steals the show.

Gettin' Jiggy Wit It: Fashion and Hip Hop Consumerism

The June 1997 issue of the *Source* magazine, one of the most recognized print media exclusively dealing with hip hop culture, had a feature of the rap group Wu-Tang Clan. While the issue's focus is the popular Staten Island rap group, a reader would have to flip past 67 full-page ads, twenty-nine from clothing companies alone (George, 1998). In the August 1997 issue of *Vibe*, another well respected hip hop bugle, there were ninety-three full page ads, twenty-six of them clothing ads. It is clear that the fashion industry has gained much profit from hip hop's rising success.

Apparel companies have always capitalized on youth trends. They research what studies say about youth development and they quickly change marketing strategies to match the reports. For example, studies show that in their quest to be accepted by peers, many adolescents dress in ways that specifically identify them as members of a particular group (Kasser & Kanner, 2004). Clothing articles must be worn by famous artists first (read hip hop icons) before adolescents are socially allowed to adopt the trend. One study reports that Black adolescents' decisions to purchase expensive sneakers were influenced by Black celebrity endorsements. Another report stated that marketers package the images of Black celebrities so that their images can be "co-branded" with a given product. Therefore, any item worn or consumed in front of peers without the stamp of approval from their favorite celebrity/hip hop artist/product endorser can be a potential fashion risk (Siegel, Coffey, & Livingston, 2001). Adolescents are extremely concerned with wearing and consuming the right brands in order to gain peer acceptance. It is no surprise, therefore, that as hip hop culture began to permeate youth culture, designers took their design cues from the collective genre. The collective genre, however, was taking their fashion cues from the federal penitentiary.

Prison policies give birth to hip hop fashion trends

The quintessential, hip hop fashion look includes sagging blue jeans. Most adolescents, of every racial group, do not know that this fashion trend originated in prisons. Jails stopped issuing belts in the 1970s because inmates were hanging themselves with the garment. So, if a gaunt inmate was issued a pair of extra large pants, he had no choice but to let them sag. This is the same reason why prisons stopped issuing sneakers with shoelaces, which also became a fad (in the early years of hip hop, most people who donned Adidas sneakers did so without the laces). Considering the millions of African American men that have been incarcerated over the past 3 decades, it is interesting that companies have taken this community epidemic and morphed it into fashion styles that are sold in malls and shops across mainstream America.

Exploiting the hip hop culture

The commodification of African American culture has occurred for decades. Prior to the 1980s, however, manufacturers did not view the Black *youth* market as profitable (Kasser & Kanner, 2004). That all changed with the birth of hip hop. The new genre gave companies an opportunity to create innovative ways to reach the hip hop community.

The earliest, most memorable moment that highlights the relationship between hip hop, fashion, and consumerism occurred in 1986. Run-D.M.C, managed by Russell Simmons, was headlining at a concert in New York City's Madison Square Garden arena. There were potential endorsers (Adidas executives from Germany) standing off-stage when Run-D.M.C. prepared to perform their song "My Adidas" (George, 1998). To open up the song, Run told the crowd to hold up their Adidas sneakers; most of the crowd had the three-striped athletic sneaker in hand. When Run walked offstage that night the Adidas representatives told him that he could have his own line of Adidas clothing; within a year, Adidas and the group's management company

negotiated a deal for $1.5 million dollars. This endorsement deal took hip hop consumerism to a brand new level. Rappers were not only taking the styles from the streets and promoting them in music videos; they were now having major manufacturers tailor create commodities for them.

The concert arena proved profitable for other fashion gurus as well. Charles Stettler, the manager of a popular, 1980s hip hop group called the Fat Boys, convinced the Swiss makers of Swatch watches to underwrite a national hip hop tour for the group (George, 1998). For the mid 80s, this was a significant breakthrough for hip hop in terms of corporate sponsorship, giving national exposure to a still somewhat community-oriented genre.

Another example of hip hop and fashion consumerism involves Tommy Hilfiger. Fashion trends, have increasingly shown that Black and White youth are taking fashion cues from each other; some White, middle-class youth, for example, wear the traditional Black hip hop dress (e.g. low-hung baggy pants and oversized shirts) and some Black youth wear typical, suburban, White college-prep dress (e.g. polo shirts and oxford shoes). Tommy Hilfiger capitalized off this trend by creating an *urban prep* look that hip hop artists as early as A Tribe Called Quest and as recent as Kanye West have donned (Kasser & Kanner, 2004).

The Tommy Hilfiger corporation has made lucrative profits targeting hip hop consumers (specifically Black youth) with the invention of the urban prep look. Initially, the company solely marketed preppy apparel associated with a lifestyle of leisure and class. Hilfiger, with the help of hip hop artists, realized that working-class Black youth were attracted to this look because of the status it portrayed. As a result, he created a fashion line specifically designed for the hip hop-driven youth market. Kids said they wanted his logos larger, more plentiful, and more colorful. He happily obliged and created the urban prep line that combined the prep-school look with a loose, baggy feel (George, 1998)

Rappers, such as Grand Puba and Chef Raekwon, wore the new line and frequently mentioned *Tommy Hill* in songs. Snoop Doggy Dog wore a Hilfiger shirt during his performance on Saturday Night Live and the next day stores across the country were sold out. (Twitchell, 1994). These artists publicized the Hilfiger-hip hop matrimony in such a way that led other rappers, industry personnel, and active consumers straight to the new look, thereby increasing fashion consumerism within the hip hop community (George, 1998). As a result of hip hop's influence and teens desire to imitate celebrated hip hop artists, Hilfiger corporate sales went from

$53 million in 1991 to $847 million in 1998 (Kasser & Kanner, 2004). In 1996 it was the number-one apparel company traded on the New York Stock Exchange (George, 1998).

Fortune 500 companies (like Adidas and Tommy Hilfiger) were not the only ones to commodify hip hop. Local businesses also played a role in hip hop fashion consumption. Dapper Dan's, a hip hop boutique in Harlem, New York, was an early contributor to the hip hop fashion scene. Artists like Eric B. & Rakim patronized the store; their faux Gucci outfits worn on the cover of their album *Follow the Leader* were hand stitched at Dapper Dan's (George, 1998). Many other designer emblems, including Louis Vuitton and Fendi, were embossed on various materials to give hip hoppers the illusion of style and class.

As hip hop became more popular in mainstream America, artists began to gain financial success, thereby increasing conspicuous consumption. As a result, many hip hop adolescents are obsessed with having expensive, designer, brand-labeled, or celebrity-endorsed dress (Kasser & Kanner, 2004). They have fully accepted America's cultural ethos that equates material possessions with beauty, power, and success.

The appropriation of high fashion items in hip hop began in the late 1970s with *Cazals*, a line of designer glasses; they were frames worn without any glass (George, 1998). It graduated in the 1990s with rappers like Foxy Brown and Lil' Kim supporting, flaunting, and advertising designers like Dolce and Gabana and Versace, respectively. Throngs of hip hop lovers, even teens, became consumers of the high-priced commodities.

In order for apparel companies (high-end and low-end) to successfully market their products, they must research trends. How much of this research, though, especially of African American fashion, borders exploitation? With the help of big businesses, common items worn by youth, especially Black youth, have become mainstream fashion trends within the hip hop community. The *do-rag*, for example, is headgear commonly worn by Black youth to set and keep hair in place, prior to dressing to go out (Kasser & Kanner, 2004). It has been used for decades, but has evolved from a discarded, cut up, female stocking (usually inexpensive or free), to a polyester piece of cloth (sold for $2-4), to an elastic-banded cap, marketed in a variety of colors with a brand label (sold for $8-20). Marketers are successfully targeting Black adolescent males, many of whom are hip hop consumers. But is this common practice equivalent to exploitation or could it simply be a lack of consumer power?

"Fight the Power": Consumer Power within the Hip Hop Community

Although hip hop consumerism has been rampant for decades, and shows no signs of relenting, there are a few examples of consumer power, where individual artists/the hip hop community at-large stood strong against corporate giants.

For a long time, the official boot of the hip hop community was Timberland. One could see "Tims" (as they are affectionately called) worn in music videos, on stage, and in the streets. Worn throughout the calendar year, Timberland boots were made popular by crack dealers working urban street corners (George, 1998). The style, however, disappeared from hip hop culture when word got out that the company was unpleased with the brand's association with hip hop culture and urban youth. Hip hop artists unofficially boycotted the boot, thereby demonstrating consumer power amongst hip hop artists and subsequently amongst hip hop adolescent consumers.

Another example of hip hop consumer power is when Chuck D filed a $5 million lawsuit against the malt liquor-makers St. Ides (Quinn, 2005). He was livid when, in 1991, a St. Ides radio commercial sampled his voice without permission. He put the spotlight on the company by writing a song called "1 Million Bottlebags." In the song he criticized companies that profited from the pains of African Americans, while challenging black people to take control of their consumer power. He was so successful in his rally against the St. Ides' makers that they made a public commitment to donate at least $100,000 per year to African American-oriented community projects.

It is hard, however, for hip hop artists to strike out against corporations and risk losing earning power through endorsement and record deals. The duality that most hip hop artists struggle with— pain versus profit —is evident in artist Chuck D. Although he was instrumental in denouncing corporate exploitation, he also struggled with the overwhelming desire to make money. Chuck D did not only criticize St. Ides (as previously mentioned); he also condemned Nike. In this example, however, he later promoted them.

In his book *Fight the Power: Rap, Race, and Reality*, Chuck D tried to justify doing a Nike commercial voice-over, despite previously criticizing Nike in his song "Shut 'Em Down." Chuck D defended himself by stating that he liked Nike but felt they should put more substantial

39

resources back into the African American community since they were such heavy supporters of the company (42). He went on to say that although some Black leaders were organizing a boycott against Nike for its insufficient community support, he doesn't believe in boycotts: "The best way to boycott is to build your own" (42). Although it sounds like nice rhetoric, it is clear that consumerism, at its best, easily defeats social consciousness.

Chuck D is not the only rapper to struggle with capitalism versus social responsibility. Although demonstrations of consumer power occasionally occur, it is definitely the exception and not the rule. Hip hop is a business and most artists are most concerned with making money. There are a few hip hop artists that do not want to help corporations exploit their communities, but the American ideals of wealth, greed, and individualism usually win. Rapper Ice Cube said in an interview, early in his career, that although corporations that represent commodities like St. Ides are "anti-everything that everybody [stands] for" we should use them as stepping stones to community development (Quinn, 2005). He referenced St. Ides' $100,000 yearly donation to Black community organizations: "How else could the Black community come up with [that kind of money] to help an organization?"

Don't Believe The Hype: Social Consciousness and Hip Hop

Unfortunately, that sentiment looms large within the hip hop world. Alternatives to mainstream consumption are considered unprofitable. Social consciousness and the desire to make money seem to be polarities that can not co-exist within hip hop artists. Even in the era of hip hop known as *political rap* (late 1980s), consumption still reigned. Although Public Enemy made politics seem cool, they also made it a commodity (George, 1998). Hip hop artists are not social activists by training or inclination. The commodification of hip hop would never allow artists to wander too far away from their main objective— to make and sell records: "While hip hop's values are by and large fixed— its spirit of rebellion, identification with street culture, materialism, and aggression— it is also an incredibly flexible tool of communication, quite adaptable, to any number of messages. That's one reason it has endured…That's why it has been so easy to turn every element of the culture associated with hip hop into a product…." (George, 1998). It is true that hip hop can function as a tool to increase political awareness, but its survival depends on its ability to change foci (according to consumer trends and the buying public).

Hip hop is first and foremost a business. Rappers have messages they would like to share with their largely adolescent fan-base. Larger corporations, though, control the distribution channels. In most cases, this forces hip hop artists to come to terms with what is seen by corporate-owned recording studios as currently marketable in order to secure any serious level of mass distribution. This pressures rappers to maintain a style and image that may compromise their personal values (Kitwana, 2005). Popular rap artist and CEO of Terror Squad Records Fat Joe said that if he could make one sweeping change in hip hop he would want the radio program directors to give radio back to hip hop. An artist wouldn't have to be associated with an already established rapper in order to get airplay. Artists could be true to their craft and not be concerned with making, packaging, and marketing commercialized music. Kitwana concurs and says "as long as rap artists depend exclusively on the corporate-controlled, market-driven recording industry and economic elite-influenced mass media, their images will be distorted" (Kitwana, 2005). The commercialization of rap music has made many rappers financially successful, but simultaneously constricted the voice of the rapper's themselves and the community from which they emerge:

> Hip hop has the potential to revolutionize but instead has been co-opted by companies, advertisers, and marketers. Talented hip hop artists that rap about social change and community uplifting stay local (read underpaid), while rappers that promote consumerist values sell platinum albums. Hip Hop's capitalism is asserted as a black populist capitalism that exists as a desire for the acquisition of wealth, but also as a desire to "stick it" to American economic and social inequities. And ultimately, hip hop artists, even at their most wealthy more often than not are at the mercy of and exploited by big-business capitalism for their continued economic success [sic]. [Most] professional hip hop artists are not wealthy and find themselves in unfair recording contracts or paid in luxury items and so seduced into debt to the record company. Only a small number of record companies actually owned by artists are not subsidiaries of larger labels that exercise ultimate control. Most of the time artists are not experiencing the wealth they rhyme about (Perry, 2004).

Even hip hop mogul Russell Simmons admitted that he routinely inflated the revenues of his clothing company Phat Farm to make the apparel seem more popular than it really was. In a court deposition he stated, "It is how you develop an image for companies... you give out false statements to mislead the public so they will then increase in their minds the value of your company" (Oliver & Leffel, 2006).

There is a double-consciousness that exists within the hip hop community. Dedicated hip

hop fans see the commercialization of hip hop as selling out. Unfortunately, however, the road to financial success often involves compromising the message of the music and celebrating consumerism and capitalism. Loyal fans want the musical genre to be more than partying and spending money, but the music is of this American culture. Our national culture reifies mediocrity, sensation, and flashiness over skill and excellence in everything from movies and television to literature and music (Perry, 2004). Hip hop has morphed into the perfect replica of American culture, capitalism and all.

The Revolution Will Not Be Televised: Solutions for a Commodified Culture

It is true that hip hop consumerism has corroded adolescent culture, but there are several ways to reverse the trend. One way is to use hip hop culture as a tool for educational advancement. There are several scholars involved in hip hop curriculum development. John Baugh, for example, a linguistics expert who focuses on African American Vernacular English, proposes that we use the orality of music and transfer it into increased literacy skills. Many inner-city students are bored with traditional reading materials. In efforts to motivate these students towards increased literacy Baugh created a series of games called *Lyric Shuffle*; it is patterned after "follow the bouncing ball" as featured in many reading programs. He designed this game to introduce and reinforce literacy through highly motivational exercises incorporating popular lyric music (Baugh, 1999). Black students are similar to all American students in the sense that popular music plays a major role in their lives. Why not use their interest in hip hop culture to increase literacy?

There are several companies that have taken this idea and treat it as the latest commodity. A book featured on MTV, for example, uses a hip hop approach to vocabulary building in preparation for the SAT. *Flocabulary* is full of song lyrics with advanced vocabulary words that can be recited to a hip-hop beat; a compact disc is included for rhythmic accompaniment (Harrison & Rappaport, 2006). The lyrics are followed by activities such as synonym matching, sentence completion, and reading comprehension. The following is an example of one verse in the hip hop vocabulary development book: "Me without a mic is like a plant without water/ It grows limp and flaccid / I get flabbergasted and astounded. " The idea of using hip hop lingo to increase SAT scores is not a new development; it has simply been commodified and sold to the general public. It would be much more beneficial to take these

42

innovative strategies and *de-commodify* them. There are academicians and community/social activists bridging the gap between hip hop and education where empowerment, not profitability, is the goal (www.h2ed.net).

The Global Youth Action Network is an excellent example of one existing vehicle that can facilitate youth participation in every sector. They are successful in mobilizing adolescents towards increased empowerment, not increased consumerism, and their sole purpose is to improve social consciousness within the adolescent community. In one protest they traveled to New York City's Time Square where they tried to use MTV's popular show *Total Request Live* as a vehicle to reach the teenage mass. The hour-long music request program regularly pans down to the street level where adolescents from all over the country wait for their chance of a cameo shot. Usually kids hold signs that promote the show, but a group of adolescents from the Global Youth Action Network held signs of a different nature (Quart, 2003). They read: "New Yorkers Say No to War, Youth Wants Peace, It's Our Future, Carson." This action shows that adolescents are aware that music and its influence on youth culture can be used as a platform to address social issues. Adults (whether television executives, apparel CEOs, or rap artists) should take note and stop exploiting hip hop's influence for financial gain; instead, use its popularity to raise awareness about issues that affect youth in America, as well as youth globally. Yes, it is true that cash rules everything around us. But maybe more people will see that the hip hop culture can transcend its current arena. Maybe not Viacom (MTV security guards quickly ended the youth protest by telling them that they were standing on private property and could only be carrying signs that had to do with *TRL)*, but hopefully someone (Quart, 2003).

Consumerism and conspicuous consumption have become fundamental elements within the hip hop culture. Unfortunately, corporations have been predators and adolescents have been prey. For teens, hip hop is a lifestyle, a symbol of freedom and rebellion for urban, suburban, and rural teens alike (Zollo, 2004). Although America's youth have been struggling for decades in core content areas, lacking basic skills and falling short compared to their international peers, one thing is certain. The hip hop culture has helped adolescents score an A+ in art: the art of consumption.

References

Artists of the Year. (2005, December/January) *Teen People*.

Top 10 Celeb Disses: 50 Cent vs. Ja Rule. (2005, September). *Teen People*.

50 Cent. 2005. *From pieces to weight*. New York: Pocket Books.

Anyon, J. (2005). *Radical possibilities: Public policy, urban education, and a new social movement*. New York: Routledge.

Baugh, J. (1999). *Out of the mouths of slaves: African American language and educational malpractice*. Austin: University of Texas Press.

Chuck D. (1997). *Fight the power: Rap, race, and reality*. New York: Delacorte Press.

Epstein, J.S. (1994). Misplaced childhood: An introduction to the sociology of youth and their music. In J.S. Epstein (Ed.), *Adolescents and their music: If it's too loud, you're too old* (pp. xiii-xxxiv). New York: Garland Publishing.

George, N. (1998). *Hip hop America*. New York: Viking.

Gunter, B. & Furnham, A. (1998). *Children as consumers: A psychological analysis of the young people's market*. London: Routledge.

Harrison, B. & Rappaport, A. (2006). *Flocabulary: The hip hop approach to SAT-level vocabulary building*. Kennebunkport: Cider Mill.

Kitwana, B. (2005). *Why white kids love hip-hop: Wankstas, wiggers, wannabes, and the new reality of race in America*. New York: Basic Civitas.

LaPoint, V.D. & Hambrick-Dixon, P.J. (2004). Commercialism's influence on black youth: The case of dress-related challenges. In T. Kasser & A.D. Kanner (Eds.), *Psychology and consumer culture: The struggle for a good life in a materialistic world* (pp. 233-250). Washington, DC:

American Psychological Association.

Morgan, J. (1999). *When chickenheads come home to roost: A hip-hop feminist breaks it down.* New York: Touchstone.

Oliver, R. & Leffel, T. (2006). *Hip-hop inc.: Success strategies of the rap moguls.* New York: Thunder's Mouth Press.

Perry, I. (2004). *Prophets of the hood: Politics and poetics in hip-hop.* Durham: Duke University Press.

Quart, A. (2003). *Branded: The buying and selling of teenagers.* Cambridge: Perseus Publishing.

Quinn, E. (2005). *Nuthin' but a "G" thang: The culture and commerce of gangsta rap.* New York: Columbia University Press.

Schor, J.B. (2004). *Born to buy: The commercialized child and the new consumer culture.* New York: Scribner.

Siegel, D.L., Coffey, T.J., & Livingston, G. (2001). *The great tween buying machine: Marketing to today's tweens.* Ithaca: Paramount Market Publishing.

Springhall, J. (1998). *Youth, popular culture and moral panics: Penny gaffs to gangsta rap, 1830-1996.* New York: St. Martin's Press.

Twitchell, J.B. (1999). *Lead us into temptation: The triumph of American materialism.* New York: Columbia University Press.

Wartella, E. & Mazzarella, S. (1990). A historical comparison of children's use of leisure time. In R. Butsch (Ed.), *For fun and profit: The transformation of leisure into consumption.* Philadelphia: Temple University Press.

Zollo, P. (2004). *Getting wiser to teens: More insights into marketing to teenagers.* Ithaca: New Strategist Publications.

David Stovall, Ph.D.
Assistant Professor
Policy Studies and African-American Studies
University of Illinois at Chicago
Hip-Hop and Social Studies for Critical Analysis

As educators, activists, community organizers, and concerned community members, one of the most important, yet neglected spaces for critically engaging young people is their own world-view. In this day and age, critical content can be developed through hip-hop. In so doing, the remainder of this brief document seeks to address a particular question: can hip-hop, as an element of popular culture, be utilized as a central theme in developing critical analysis in a secondary social studies classroom. Where hip-hop has been castigated in the popular media for its controversial lyrics and presuppositions, the remainder of this text locates hip-hop as a transformative element in the development of critical teaching and thinking. Although not considered a mainstream element of popular culture in its inception during the late seventies, hip-hop music and culture have developed into an international phenomenon critically centered in youth popular culture. As teachers concerned with developing critical learning search for new and innovative ways to introduce educational relevance, hip-hop should be located in the range of approaches. Developing relationships based on familiarity and importance, students have the greater propensity to grasp concepts originally considered foreign or "uninteresting." As we often blame urban youth for society's ills (i.e. crime, drug-use, delinquency, apathetic behavior towards education, etc.), the following document offers an approach to promote critical inquiry amongst high school students.

Essentially, instead of speaking to the uses of the elements of hip-hop (DJ-ing, breakdancing, graf-writing, MC-ing, beatboxing, doing the knowledge, etc.) as stagnant text, the following account is written from my perspective as a high school social studies teacher in Chicago. Where the songs I use for this section are quite dated, they do however speak to the various uses of hip-hop as text to be problematized, critiqued, and discussed in a high school social studies classroom.

47

My high school social studies course is based on critical inquiry. Heavily centered in dialogue and action research projects, I engage my students with numerous questions on their lives and community. Using hip-hop lyrics as text, I wanted to develop a critical inquiry focusing on the differences between "school" and "education." From previous discussions, "school" was viewed as the process young people were subjected to reproduce the social order (status quo). "Education" as a completely different process, was understood to be the process by which members of the society are able to process, engage, question, and change their realities, on both personal and collective levels. From this space, the students developed questions to distinguish the difference between school and education. Some of the questions we asked were: How did school promote deception? Where did they feel the dishonesty to occur? How should students respond to dishonesty? Were we as facilitators/teachers cooperating in promoting the deception? Knowing what they know now, what would they change in their current institution? Where many would see the following set of questions to be dangerous for a high school social studies class, I embraced it as a form of critical inquiry.

Over the semester, many of the students responded that they were starting to feel that they had been deceived in the years before. Not to divert their concerns, I introduced another song by an East Coast rap group considered to be "underground" (outside of the scope of mainstream media). Respected amongst hip-hop aficionados for their lyrical content and quality sound, Reflection Eternal's (Talib Kweli and DJ Hi-Tek) "Four Women" provides a segue way to the relevance of history. A rendition of a jazz tune by vocalist and pianist Nina Simone, Four Women tells the story of four women's experience during slavery. Each verse tells a story of one woman's experience in relationship to the color of her skin. The darkest woman (Aunt Sarah) recalls her experience as a field hand. The lightest (Zaphronia) tells the story of being the offspring of a plantation owner and a bondswoman. The two women in between (Sweet Thing and Peaches) speak of resistance and the shame felt from the experience of slavery. The story of Aunt Sarah was of particular relevance in this juncture to the theme of deception. Here the class engages in a story often omitted in high school history or social studies class.

...her skin is Black like it was packed with melanin

back in the days of slaves she'd be packin' like Harriet Tubman

and

her arms are long and they move like a song

feet with corns hands with calluses

but the heart is warm...

the headwrap is a remedy

and her back is strong and

she's far from a vagabond

this is the back the master's whip

used to crack upon

strong enough to take all the pain that's been afflicted

again, and again, and again, and flip it

to be there for her children

nothin' else matters

what do they call her

they call her Aunt Sarah (T.K. Greene, 2001)

The class was challenged with the question: What would be included in a curriculum that challenged dishonesty? Here the deception lies in the status quo view of history, where the contributions of those outside the White Anglo-Saxon paradigm are excluded. Students would often reveal that they would become disinterested because much of the course material in history and social studies class would not be reflective of their experiences in the United States.

Returning to the assignment, students began to roam around the class and pick out books, articles, and internet sources. As a continuing project, the challenge for the class was to create a curriculum and propose it to the school at the end of the year. After students contributed with exercises and texts they felt would promote accuracy in curriculum, we engaged in dialogue surrounding Howard Zinn's (1997) A People's History of the United States. Written with the premise of getting students to "think for themselves" Zinn's text provides multiple viewpoints in engaging history (Zinn 1997, p.xi). His chapter "Slavery without Submission, Emancipation without Freedom," highlights the contributions of abolitionist's resistance to slavery. Committed to critical analysis in history, the same chapter demystifies Lincoln as a benevolent president devoted to the well being of African-Americans. Lyrics in the Reflection Eternal song, although not critical of Lincoln, can be utilized as a bridge to introduce students to alternative views in the historical record. Although a small example, we are able to develop strategies by which to enhance student engagement through critical analysis.

Marcella Runell

Doctoral Candidate

University of Massachusetts, Amherst

The Organic Connection Between Hip-Hop and Social Justice Education

It is estimated that over two hundred classes on Hip-Hop are being offered at colleges and universities throughout the United States and abroad. At present, there are currently Hip-Hop Archives at both Harvard and Stanford Universities. Both Howard University, after becoming the first university to bring Hip-Hop to the Academy in 1991, as well as Carlton College, will soon offer Hip-Hop studies as a minor. In August 2006, in Chemnitz, Germany, in conjunction with the annual Splash! Festival, there was an International Hip-Hop Meets Academia conference drawing scholars, activists and artists from around the world. And for the first time in history the Rock-n-Roll Hall of Fame partnered with the Hip-Hop Association, a non-profit organization dedicated to the preservation of hip hop culture, to host a 2006 Summer Teacher Institute entitled: Elevate! Using Hip-Hop to Educate. Hip-Hop's takeover of the academy is no surprise; it represents growing numbers of Hip-Hop heads turned Hip-Hop scholars.

Hip-Hop music and culture have become a global phenomenon because Hip-Hop is a powerful cultural art form that can be identified as having three particular and unique strengths. Hip-Hop music and culture have the capacity to stimulate the imagination and emotion of listeners through empirical story telling. Secondly, Hip-Hop music and culture are able to create a public discourse where multiple experiences as well as multiple intelligences are valued. And, the third most important strength is that Hip-Hop music and culture act as a public, global sounding board for artists and fans to question universal attitudes about nationality, race, class, and gender representations.

Birthed in the early 1970's by and for young people of color living in urban areas of the United States, it has become the voice of youth culture worldwide with enormous potential for social and political change. Hip-Hop music provides a counter-narrative to mainstream cultural values and media influences. Today Hip-Hop music is not merely considered a form of entertainment but rather a primary language of youth that is intimately connected to variations of identity, values, and politics. Worldwide, from South Africa to Poland, and from the Bronx to Beverly Hills, the popularity and global significance of Hip-Hop music and culture has been observed and needs to be interrogated as a useful tool for educating our youth and ourselves.

Because of its promise and possibility as public pedagogy it is also useful to explore its impact in traditional educational settings. Many educators are opting to use Hip-Hop music and culture as both content and pedagogy for various types of courses including but not limited to: literature, writing, mathematics, history, social studies, and social justice education at all levels of education K-16. This paper will examine how Hip-Hop music and culture has become in effect for many educators, a critical Hip-Hop pedagogy, forging an organic connection between Hip-Hop and Social Justice Education.

I identify myself as a member of the Hip-Hop generation because of my long-standing relationship to the music and culture. Therefore it has a major influence on how I see the world, and how I experience my various social identities as an urban, white, working class, thirty-two-year old woman. And because it is a generation that I am apart of, and something that I am continually thinking about in my professional experience as a social justice educator, I believe it is useful to explore as pedagogy.

I recently resided in Amherst Massachusetts. In 2002, I made the decision to leave New York City, where I was happily pursuing a second master's degree in Africana Studies at NYU, working in the student affairs department and living blissfully in the Prospect Heights area of Brooklyn. I left because I had the opportunity to get my doctorate from the highly acclaimed Social Justice Education program at the University of Massachusetts, Amherst. During my tenure at NYU, I was influenced by and studying, with Hip-Hop intellectuals such as Robin Kelly, Tricia Rose and Nelson George. I also found that working with NYU students, primarily students of color, although not exclusively, there were many exciting opportunities for us to use Hip-Hop as the backdrop and/or focus for most of the programming efforts including: debates, leadership programs, conferences, parties, concerts, etc.

In 1997 when I first started at NYU as a graduate student, I began to witness a change in the prominence of Hip-Hop as an identity and a political force. Since I am an educator, I also realized that hip-hop having the power and strength to create an identity and a political agenda, meant Hip-Hop might also work as critical pedagogy. Although it would be sometime before I found other people who were working towards a similar goal, I felt that I was on the brink of witnessing a movement. Years later, when I entered the Social Justice Education program, I came in ready to get started proving my theory that Hip-Hop as critical pedagogy was cutting edge social justice work. I was met with a lukewarm response at best. Most of the well-intentioned faculty, asked questions such as, "Why hip-hop? Why would you study that? Is there even anything written about that? If you did an academic search will anything come up? What exactly is hip hop-if you could just tell me what it is then maybe I could understand? Isn't it all just violent and misogynistic anyway? How can you be a social justice educator and be interested in researching hip hop as an academic pursuit?" After hearing these responses, I thought-*how could I not*? How is it that a doctoral program focused on social justice education in the United States is not concerned with the connection between Hip- Hop culture and social justice education?

Ironically at the same time that I was experiencing the obvious resistance and concern about my academic pursuits, something else happened. I attended a "Hip-Hop night" at the one and only Hip-Hop "club" in Amherst. I was so happy to walk in and hear familiar music in a place that was feeling especially foreign to me. As soon as I walked in I realized- nearly everyone in the entire club (all 100 people) including the DJ- with the exception of the crew that I walked in with, were white. I had never experienced anything like that- the feeling of looking around and seeing a room full of white people singing along, to all Hip-Hop records... replete with using the "N" word unapologetically. I was stunned.

After my initial shock wore off and I began teaching undergraduate social justice education courses, I realized something that changed the direction of my work. I felt that despite the fact that the faculty and many of my colleagues didn't understand much about Hip-Hop, the UMASS students were consuming Hip-Hop without any social justice analysis at all, and that was where my belief in the organic connection between Hip-Hop and social justice education was solidified. The majority of UMASS students are white, middle class, and suburban, taking SJE courses because they fulfill general education requirements. I set to work creating first a justification for using Hip-Hop as both pedagogy and content relying on theorists such as Paulo Freire, Gloria Ladson-Billings and Sonia Nieto. Then I looked to the principles of social justice education and attempted to make the case for my belief in the organic connection between Hip-Hop as critical pedagogy and social justice education

One of the key aspects regarding the use of Hip-Hop is the benefit of using something to motivate and stimulate students, which is relevant to their every day lives. Sonia Nieto writes in her article, "Critical Multicultural Education and Students' Perspectives" that in relation to the content in education, students are eager to express opinions regarding both the tangible curriculum which is the obvious content, as well as the covert "hidden" curriculum. Nieto cites a particular study, which revealed that over a third of the students found that *none* of the course content related to their lives outside of the classroom. Nieto stresses that a successful component of critical multicultural education is when teachers take an active role in learning about their students' backgrounds and lives. Hip-Hop is a critical piece in how this works, because it is a powerful influence over students, which could help the teachers to learn more about various cultural and environmental conditions influencing their students, which in turn would likely create a more active learning environment. Hip-Hop also enables students to learn through their ability tell their stories via the music or listen to other stories told through the music. Hip-Hop is intrinsically a medium that allows stories to be told about struggle and overcoming obstacles related to race, class, gender, religion and other forms of oppression. (Nieto, 1999)

"It (critical multicultural education) is not neat; it does not have all the answers." (Nieto, 1999, p.207) And like critical multicultural education, Hip-Hop does not provide all the answers but it is a place to start in meeting the needs of students who long to be affirmed in a genuine way. These practical applications of critical multicultural education can also be connected to Social Justice Education principles which are derived from multiple pedagogical traditions and epistemologies including: laboratory and intergroup education, community organizing, women' studies, black studies, adult literacy education, experiential learning, and social and cognitive development models. (Adams, 1997, p. 30) Social Justice Education principles include:

- Social Justice Education seeks to balance the emotional and cognitive components of the learning process. For many students using a Hip-Hop pedagogy allows them to begin

healing by using the texts of artists who have experienced many of the societal ills that plague urban students. Hip Hop serves as a healing agent for many; a catharsis of pent-up emotion, and alternative to acting out violently.

- Social Justice Education acknowledges and supports the personal (the individual student's experience) while illuminating the systemic (the interactions among social groups). Hip-Hop tends to tell stories that make the societal issues personal. Detailed references about drugs, crime, and of other interpersonal conflicts and dysfunction are uniquely dominant in Hip-Hop. (Perry, 2004, p.7)

- Social Justice Education attempts to attend to social relations in the classroom. Because of the co-option and commercialization of Hip-Hop across the United States and around the world, using it as pedagogy to discuss group dynamics such as behavior associated with internalized oppression without blaming or judging individual students could be a tangible strategy. In addition Hip-Hop tends to very descriptive and may give students a voice or language to talk about their feelings in a more open way through poetry or other art forms associated with Hip-Hop.

- Social Justice Education utilizes reflection and experience as tools for student-centered learning. "Teaching that begins from the student's world view and experiences as the starting point for dialogue or problem posing." (Adams, 1997, p.43) Hip-Hop for many students it their primary world view influencing what they wear, how they speak, what they read, what video games they play, what TV shows they watch, what movies to they attend, what music they listen to and who they admire as a leader.

- Social Justice Education values awareness, personal growth and change as outcomes of the learning process. "Hip-Hop allows for brilliant insights into human relationships and into existence in a society mired in difficult race and gender politics which is often becomes economically exploitative and exclusive." (Perry, 2004, p.8) Students want to be able to tell their story, reflect on their story and learn how to take action.

Joan Wink, in her book, *Critical Pedagogy: Notes from the Real World*, defines critical pedagogy as being able to name, to reflect critically, and to act. (Wink, 2005, p.23) But she stresses, "I doubt I can teach someone how to do critical pedagogy. We do not *do* critical pedagogy; we live it. Critical pedagogy is not a method; it is a way of life." (Wink, 2005, p. 120) I believe the same to be true of Hip Hop as pedagogy, if this methodology speaks to you as an educator because of who you are and/or because of who your students are, then it is an organic connection and will likely bring a great deal of success to your educational practice. There are many people out in the field who are already doing "it."

The definition of Social Justice Education (SJE) is working towards a society that includes full and equal participation for all groups. (Adams, 1997) Social Justice Education principles, which are derived from multiple pedagogical traditions and epistemologist, inadvertently in many ways support the use of hip-hop as critical pedagogy. (Adams, 1997, p. 30) All social justice education courses begin with a foundational approach to teaching about oppression, using an institutional, cultural and individual lens to discuss historical and contemporary manifestations of oppression. All SJE courses also attempt to make the material relevant to individual students' experiences in order to move the students to a place where they are ready to create action plans and change strategies. Students are introduced to concepts such as collusion, internalized oppression, white privilege, appropriation, social power, and explicit definitions of racism, classism, sexism, heterosexism, anti-Semitism, and ableism. It seemed to me that Hip-Hop as critical pedagogy would be the perfect vehicle to move them to a place of greater awareness and a call to action regarding most these terms and issues.

As mentioned earlier, Hip-Hop for many students is their primary world view influencing what they wear, how they speak, what they read, what video games they play, what TV shows they watch, what movies they attend, what music they listen to and who they admire as leaders. Giving students the opportunity to deconstruct their worldview using their own Hip-Hop texts or chosen hip-hop texts is helpful in developing a more self-aware and conscious worldview. Priya Parmar, professor at Brooklyn College, co-author of *Hip Hop in the Classroom* (forthcoming), has conducted research that actually proves that using hip hop in schools has changed student's attitudes about literacy and learning, by helping students feel connected. "Educators who incorporate the teaching of hip hop culture legitimate and validate their students' culture, voice, knowledge, experiences, and histories as well as aid in the healthy construction of student's own racial and cultural identities." (Personal Correspondence, June 2006)

"Human activity consists of action and reflection: it is praxis; it is transformative of the world." (Freire, 2002, p.125) Hip-Hop music and culture has transformed the world and continues to shape attitudes about race, class and gender roles. In spring 2004, I combined my appreciation for Hip-Hop into the designs of both the undergraduate Racism and Sexism weekend workshops as part of a course that I co-taught called *Education 392: Social Justice Issues in Education*. I believe both weekends were significantly enhanced and the students strongly identified with the relevance of the messages around cultural and institutional oppression specific to racism and sexism found using Hip-Hop as a medium. However, some social justice educators may believe that my choice to use Hip-Hop in the classroom is risky and perhaps too radical, but it can certainly make education more interesting as Paulo Freire urges, "radicalization, nourished by a critical spirit, is always creative." (Freire, 2002, p. 115)

My personal experience using Hip-Hop in the classroom as a social justice educator *has* made me feel like a radical in many situations. Prior to teaching the undergraduate racism workshop I was feeling somewhat uninspired by the choices available to illustrate how the media perpetuates racism. It is a topic that I am constantly thinking about and know that it has a huge influence on student values and perceptions of race, but I wasn't sure how to bring that out in class. It seemed that many of the usual suspects such as "Killing Us Softly" seemed to be losing some of their power within the UMASS undergraduate population since so many other departments from communication to sociology have used the same videos. So I went on my own search and during February as a salute to Black History Month, VH1 ran a special called, *Ego Trips: Illest Minority Moments*. It is an hour-long video showing how people of color are systematically targeted and placed in subordinate roles in every aspect of television from reality TV to cartoons to professional wrestling and sitcoms-past and present. The various commentators are all people of color who are part of the Hip-Hop generation, with the exception of one white man who is a rapper/writer/activist. Other commentators were Hip-Hop artists, writers, comedians, scholars and activists.

Prior to showing the video I screened it with a group of current SJE students. They found it to be sexist, offensive, violent, too much insider-humor, a generational difference for the current students; non-SJE language was being used, etc. Overall they recommended that my co-facilitator and I did not use it, and if we did it should only be used in small clips. However, we decided to proceed with the video, naming the dynamics we had tracked explicitly to the students, and allowing the students to make meaning of the video themselves. Three important factors that we considered were: 1) it was already currently airing on VH1 so there was a good chance that many of the students, particularly students of color and white students in intimate friendship and relationship with people of color had already seen all or part of it 2) the overall content and footage depicting cultural racism was exceptional and provided so much to talk about 3) the video was meant to create a space for critical dialogue and discussion, not meant to be a definitive look at race and the media. Needless to say the students cited it as one of the most "important," "influential," "eye-opening" and "innovative" aspects of the weekend. All of the students vowed to take another look at cartoons, talk shows, and sitcoms they had previously been "sleep-walking" through. This was reflected in their evaluations and personal reflection papers. I believe this is a good example of "popular education" and Hip-Hop as pedagogy.

The second activity utilizing Hip-Hop as pedagogy involved the use of music videos for the undergraduate sexism weekend. I recorded six music videos shown on MTV2 at 5pm on the Friday before the weekend. Five out of the six videos were Hip-Hop videos. There was no predetermined type of music; it was a *random* selection of music. I believe the heavy influence of Hip-Hop (5 out of 6 videos) speaks to the powerful influence of Hip-Hop music on youth culture. We then viewed the videos the second day of the workshop. It is important to note that we viewed the videos the second day because we had done a substantial amount of work around language, theory, and framework to understand the levels and types of sexism in society. We then asked the students to watch each video and take notice of particular dynamics around gender roles. Afterwards we broke them into subgroups by video and gave them newsprint to write down their ideas, thoughts and observations. It was amazing how most of the students who have seen these videos countless times, really saw them for the first time in many ways. As a supplement I did some background work on the artist's ages and ethnicities in case there were questions regarding the context of the video (and there were questions!). The analysis and conversation was truly phenomenal. We literally couldn't get them to stop talking and break for lunch. Many students made the point that critically viewing the media was a practical skill that they could take away with them as a step toward ending oppressive attitudes and behavior.

In a longer version of the activity I would have also given out the song lyrics which can be found at www.ohhla.com and I would have had them watch the videos a second time without the sound. Overall the group reported very similar findings to the racism participants. They loved the activity and felt "stimulated," "engaged" and "empowered" by the space to discuss, criticize and dialogue with each other. Many of them vowed to create spaces with friends and roommates around some of the "new" ideas and perspectives that they gained during the activity. On a side-note it is fascinating that twenty-eight people watching a video can actually have twenty-eight different impressions. Many people saw different semiotics, which represented to them more coded examples of sexism such as a particular expression or cultural reference. Overall it was a powerful activity.

Other examples include using Jadakiss's song "Why?" and asking graduate education students to work in groups to use newsprint to brainstorm key examples of institutional racism and classism found in the song, as well as examples of internalized oppression and how they might use the song as critical pedagogy. I showed the video first with the sound, then a second time without sound and also with the lyrics in front of them. Students then broke into small groups to pinpoint examples of the levels and types of oppression that we learned about earlier. It was a controversial lesson because of the age differences within the group and the response to the language used in the song, but also helpful to many of the people who had negative stereotypes about Hip-Hop music and culture. Other examples of using Hip-Hop texts as part of Social Justice Education courses include: using an episode of the UPN show, *Girlfriends*, called *Sister, Sista* where one of the characters' white sister comes to visit the four women of color and has completely appropriated and created her own version of a "Black identity". This provides for a provocative discussion about white privilege, appropriation, mythical norms, identity formation and identity policing, and who gets to use the "n" word. Another example is using the Dave Chappelle skit entitled the "Race Draft" to have students think about the social construction of race and racial identity politics. These are just a few abbreviated examples of the how other Hip-Hop texts can be used in social justice education courses.

More recently, in June 2006, I co-presented a new piece of the Hip-Hop education puzzle for teachers at the Rock and Roll Hall of Fame, Summer Teacher Institute, *Elevate! Using Hip-Hop to Educate*. Community activist, Shamako Noble, of the National Hip Hop Congress and I agreed, that while the teachers participating in the Institute were receiving a great deal of Hip-

Hop history, content, and information to create lessons and curriculum, they weren't necessarily being offered a social justice lens. We offered up three basic layers to consider when attempting Hip-Hop education in any form.

The first layer is that *all* Hip-Hop education should be grounded and contextualized in the belief that our society is characterized by oppression, which includes but is not limited to racism, classism and sexism. Oppression exists simultaneously on three levels, individual, cultural and institutional. In addition oppression can be unconscious (unnamed privileges) or conscious (obvious laws, policies, practices). This means that members of the Hip-Hop generation, artists and fans are socialized and influenced by the greater society in varying degrees. This also means that in order to understand Hip-Hop culture, it is important to understand social power, both in a historic and contemporary context. Hip-Hop should not be used in educational contexts without first understanding the role that oppression plays in its development and perpetuation.

The second layer of understanding regarding how to utilize Hip-Hop education is that using popular culture to reach students is Freirian in nature, and is in effect a critical pedagogy. Perhaps it is innovative to use Hip-Hop now, because of its popularity, but Freire can take the credit for a Hip-Hop pedagogy, because the principles, language and results of popular education are the foundation for Hip-Hop education. The history of critical pedagogy, is like the history of Hip-Hop, it needs to be preserved and included in the contemporary dialogue.

The third layer of the Hip-Hop education model, is comprehending the various uses of Hip-Hop in education. Hip-Hop songs, lyrics, artists, videos, or elements of Hip-Hop culture such as fashion, dancing, poetry, graffiti art, or activism, can all be useful tools in the classroom. Educators can cite a song that references police brutality as a hook to bring students into a discussion on institutional racism, or an empowering lyric from a female artist to generate a debate over gender politics, or educators can use actual videos or lyrics as text to analyze and supplement dry history or social studies curriculum. Hip-Hop education can be fine arts-based focused on learning to read or create music, sharpen poetry skills, appreciate visual arts through the history of graffiti. Hip-Hop can be supplemental, academic, artistic, or content-driven. It can be ala carte, individual lessons or whole curricula. As long as it is based on a social justice education framework, and an understanding of the nature of critical pedagogy it can also be liberatory. Without a Social Justice Education lens, using Hip-Hop will undoubtedly serve to reproduce oppressive behaviors, and ultimately duplicate the various conditions that created it in the first place.

What are the limitations of using Hip-Hop as critical pedagogy?

I realize that for some of my colleagues their relationship to and/or interest in Hip-Hop music and culture may not be organic, so to utilize these activities could create uncomfortable moments and legitimate fear of critique over the meaning and content of the material. But as Charles Beady writes, "Even teachers, who have a racial and cultural affinity with their students, often have difficulty motivating them. Young people will listen to and talk about things they are "into." Regardless of race and culture, they are into rap and hip-hop." (Beady, 2001, p. 39) So, perhaps comfort level or lack of information may be one obstacle.

The actual content and controversy embedded in Hip Hop such as the glorification of violence and/or crime, an emphasis on materialism, misogyny, homophobia, offensive language, appropriation, inability to decode what is being said, and/or feeling alienated from the culture are other legitimate concerns for educators. Hip-Hop music and culture are multi-faceted, evolving, complex, layered elements of society. Hip-Hop wasn't created to be neatly packaged for the educational system, so it is messy and often hard to work with. It can also seem contradictory at times. But it is art, which means it is always subject to critique, dialogue, and analysis. There are many different artists representing multiple viewpoints on any given issue coming from just about any place on the globe and any region of the United States. Hip-Hop is complicated and fascinating and full of potential, and certainly provides a challenge for educators who are willing to engage it to reach their students. David Stovall, Assistant Professor University of Illinois, Chicago and High School Social Studies teacher warns, "Over the next couple of years, it will be critically important for educators who use hip hop to demonstrate its necessity in the classroom. Without it [proof], another art form created by people of color will be washed away." (Personal Correspondence, May 2006)

For many educators across the United States, using Hip-Hop still feels like a radical, solitary experience. But for others, the writing is on the wall and there is an urgency to make some moves. "There is a Hip-Hop education movement right now, Kirkland emphasizes. "While it runs the risk of becoming a fad, we must continue to add fuel to 'the hip-hop education movement' because it promises real and radical social and educational change." (Personal Correspondence, May 2006) Toni Blackman, U.S. State Department Hip-Hop Ambassador, has literally traveled all over the globe educating teachers about how to maximize the use of Hip-Hop in the classroom. "When people say it's not a movement, maybe they should say 'I don't know about this movement.' (Personal Correspondence, June 2006).

How Do the Artists Weigh In?

Hip-Hop artists are not losing out on the chance to impact education in a direct way. Russell Simmons started an organization called hiphopreader.com, a youth-based literacy and leadership program that offers incentives for New York City high school students to read. Kanye West created a program called "Loop Dreams" which will put state-of-the-art music studios in at-promise areas to combat the severe dropout problem in today's high schools. Some artists are choosing to literally step up their game: rapper/producer 9th Wonder will be teaching a course on hip hop this fall at North Carolina Central University. While, Dead Prez, recently created a documentary, *It's Bigger Than Hip Hop*, which offers viewers a history lesson on Bay Area political movements. On the question of his role in hip hop and education, M-1 says, "It's our culture. It's not split in two. I see myself as a contributing factor--a freedom fighter. It's why I started rappin'. My true education came from our movement. I have seen it work inside schools, but more in the community. Schools can be authoritative, like jails. The real world education comes from observation and participation." In case you are wondering how committed these brothers are to education, M1 confirms," We are directly involved in charter schools, independent schools, for Black and Latino kids. We are always doin' fundraisers, or talking to, or providing some assistance to schools or administrators in those schools." (Personal Correspondence, June 2006)

Hip-Hop as critical pedagogy provides me with a creative praxis and more authentic teaching style. I realize this is not a universal experience for all educators. But I am interested in continuing to tell the success stories of those who are finding Hip-Hop as critical pedagogy to be transformative in working with students for whom this is a meaningful cultural expression and central to their identity.

References

Adams, M., Bell, L.E., & Griffin, P. (Eds.) (1997). *Teaching for Diversity and Social Justice: A Sourcebook.* New York: Routledge.

Beady, C. (2001). Whatever it takes 2 motivate 2-daze youth. *Education Week.* 20 (30) p.39.

Christensen, R.S. (2003). Hip Hop learning: Graffiti as an educator of urban teenagers. *Educational Foundations.* 17 (4). p.57-82.

Freire, P. (2002) *Pedagogy of the Oppressed* (30th anniversary ed.). New York: Continuum.

Kitwana, B. (2002). *The Hip Hop Generation: Young Blacks and the Crisis in African-American Culture.* New York: BasicCivitas Books.

Morrell, E. & Duncan-Andrade, J.M.R. (2002) Promoting academic literacy with urban youth through engaging hip hop culture. *English Journal.* 91 (6). P.88-92

Nieto, S. (1999). Critical Multicultural Education and Student's Perspectives. In May, S. (Ed.) *Critical Multiculturalism: Rethinking Multicultural and Antiracist Education.* (pp.191-215). London: Falmer.

Perry, I. (2004). *Prophets of the Hood: Politics and Poetics in Hip-Hop.* Durham, NC: Duke University Press.

Personal Correspondence Interviews (conducted June 2006) by Marcella Runell for VIBE magazine article

Wink, J. (2005). *Critical Pedagogy: Notes from the Real World* (3rd ed.). Boston: Pearson

Kenji Jasper

Author, Columnist, Educator

Brooklyn, New York

The Lesson 2.0

I remember the first time I used hip-hop in a classroom. Standing there, at 23, before a classroom full of night school students my age and older, I instinctively knew that these ladies and gentlemen were from a different world than I. Sure I came through the public system like most folks, through fights and jumpings and shots fired over nothing were as much a part of my life as anyone else who found adulthood at the end of the 90s, but I had seen the world. I had left my neighborhood. I had left the country. I had read books and was in the process of writing one. For me there were no limits on what I could do. But for them it was a different story. Hip hop, already my right hand man and the center of my then fledgling career, was a godsend.

I remember the day I wrote the lyrics to DMX's "Party Up" on the board, explicating each line like the work of a true poet. Beats behind the words make the message so much clearer. It's why Andre 3000, or Jadakiss, or Black Thought can convey one of my ten page concepts in ten lines. It is, for better or worse, the heart and soul of a generation born beneath its waters, drowning in both its angst and electric imagery.

So I used it as much as I could in my career as a teacher, from the images outlined in Hype William's *Belly*, to the prose of Paul Beatty, to the lyrics of everyone from Jigga to 50 Cent. Heads rose from near slumber once they knew the names. They fought for my attention through questions and answers once I spoke the language they understood, even if it wasn't the standard form mandated in our school curriculum.

The same rules apply to this new generation, one inundated with even more high-tech toys than the ones we begged for every Christmas. The fresh gear costs even more dough and even more ridiculously youthful faces than before can barely name the nine planets or the interstate they have to use to get to the next town. We're in an information age that Hip Hop America only knows because of the commercials. As the middle-class disintegrates and upper class turns their back on the masses down below there may be fewer and fewer of the classics that survive. Jay Gatsby may be forgotten. Bigger Thomas may become a memory, but somebody's gonna be singing along to "Party Up" 60 years from now. Tell the truth, who's more memorable from the 60s? James Brown (R.I.P), or Norman Mailer?

So if we're gonna teach we gotta do it in a way where we hit the bulls-eye. Does that mean every teacher should have his own DJ? Of course not. But like it or not hip hop is a bridge between who we were and what's to come, a cultural institution just strong enough to get us exactly where we need to be.

PART II: LESSON PLANS

We have included a broad range of lessons that are standards-referenced, unique, creative and easy-to-use.

I. LITERACY AND ENGLISH LANGUAGE ARTS

II. HISTORY, GLOBAL STUDIES AND GEOGRAPHY

III. MUSIC, MATH AND SCIENCE

IV. LEADERSHIP AND PEER MEDIATION

V. MEDIA AND TECHNOLOGY

VI. SOCIAL JUSTICE, TOLERANCE AND DIVERSITY

I. LITERACY AND ENGLISH ANGUAGE ARTS

> The lessons in this section include dual-language learning strategies, information about revolutionaries such as Assata Shakur, and plenty of creative writing exercises, as well as opportunities to perfect the college admissions essay.

- ### Lesson 1: Modern Momotaro: Folktales in Hip-Hop

    Author(s): Mako Fittz, Diachi Sawa, Julie Chang Schulman

- ### Lesson 2: Identifying and Utilizing Visual Language in Poetry/Narrative Writing

    Author(s): Sarah Montgomery-Glinski

- ### Lesson 3: The Story I RIGHT: Hip-Hop & Personal Narrative Writing

    Author(s): Unique Frasier

- ### Lesson 4: Listen and Write activity

    Author(s): Andrew Landers

- ### Lesson 5: Poetry Rap-Up

    Author(s): Ellen Warkentine

Did you Know:

According to a 2006 study, the United States has one of the highest literacy rates in the world. Still, approximately 3,000,000 adults cannot read or write in the United States. Imagine how many people cannot write in Niger, where less than 10% of the country can read or write. Furthermore, poverty has been proven to be in correlation with low literacy rates.

-UNESECO.ORG

-Farooq, Asmin (2006). Education: The Impact of Literacy Rates

Lesson 1: Modern Momotaro: Folktales in Hip Hop

Author(s): Mako Fitts, Daichi Sawa, Julie Chang Schulman

Bios: Mako Fittz is an Assistant Professor in the Department of Anthropology, Sociology and Social Work at Seattle University, and Affiliate Faculty in the Global African Studies and Women Studies Programs. Her research and teaching are in the areas of women's labor in entertainment industries, Black women in hip hop cultures, and issues of race, class, gender and sexuality in Black American cultures. She has published essays on the Black Clubwomen's movement of the late 19th and early 20th century and on body ethics and aesthetics among women on color.

Daichi Sawa also goes by the name Diez. Diez is an emcee/activist currently working with 206zulu and Universal Zulu Nation Japan. Locally in Seattle, Diez has a group with another emcee named Asun and they go by the name Real Talk. Real Talk is strictly focused on social awareness in their lyrics.

Julie Chang Schulman is an educator, organizer, and emcee from the crew Alpha P in Seattle, WA. She teaches English for Brain Child Learning Center, and serves as Northwest Regional Coordinator for Hip Hop Congress, Assistant Chapter Head for 206 Zulu, and Co-Director for Reclaim the Media.

Grades: 6-8, 9-12   **Subjects:** Advanced ESL, Language Arts (This lesson can also be adapted to fit a Japanese Immersion format).

Interdisciplinary Connections: Geography, Global Studies, Creative Writing

Academic Content Standards: Language Arts Standard 1- Demonstrates competence in the general skills and strategies of the writing process. Language Arts Standard 4- Gathers and uses information for research purposes. Language Arts Standard 7- Demonstrates competence in the general skills and strategies for reading a variety of informational texts. Music Standard 7- Understands the relationship between music and history and culture.

Overview of Lesson Plan: Intermediate/advanced Japanese-speaking ESL students utilize a bilingual Hip Hop song as a culturally relevant, context-embedded platform for building listening, comprehension, and spoken-fluency in English, as well as developing critical thinking skills. They will answer discussion questions and present their findings to the class along with a reading-to-rhythm recitation of the lyrics to "The Journey of Momotaro."

Note: This class is designed specifically for Japanese students, or students of other ethnicities familiar with the popular, traditional folktale "Momotaro." For integrated ESL classrooms, or for

students unfamiliar with "Momotaro," the folktale should be assigned prior to delivering this lesson.

Suggested Time Allowance: One Hour

Resources/Materials:

Paper/Pens

CD player

Song "Momotaro" by Diez, Asun, & Khazm, available online

Lyrics to "Momotaro" (included)

Activities/ Procedures:

Warm Up:

1. Explain to the students, "Today, we will be learning about Hip Hop culture through a familiar folktale."

2. Play the introduction (Japanese chorus only) to Real Talk's song "Journey of Momotaro" once or twice. Ask the students to take 5 minutes and in small groups or in partners, translate the lyrics. Then ask where the song is from. The answer is the Japanese folktale Momotaro. Distribute the traditional Momotaro handout and give the students time to look over it. Tell the students that people created folktales in part to entertain, but also to preserve their cultures by teaching each other and their children their values and beliefs through storytelling. Tell the students that today, they will be learning about Hip Hop culture through the multiracial rap group Real Talk's adaptation of Momotaro.

3. Play the full song, "The Journey of Momotaro," asking students to write down the lyrics to the best of their ability. This can be a contest to see which group can most effectively transcribe what is being said in the song.

Main Activity:

1. Break the students into small groups and distribute the lyrics to the song. Give the students time to read the lyrics, and then have them put the lyrics away (this forces to students to rely on their listening skills.) Play the song again, asking the students to take notes on content.

2. Assign each group questions to discuss.

Possible Discussion Questions:

How are good and evil represented in the Momotaro folktale?

What lessons are being taught in the story, and how are these lessons supportive of Japanese values?

Does the rap version apply different kinds of symbolism from the original folktale? What are they, and how do they differ from the original?

What is meant by *food for thought*? What do Momotaro's *mics* represent?

What is meant by *corporate celestial beings*? How is evil represented in Real Talk's song?

3. Have the groups present their findings to the rest of the class. Have the rest of the students take notes and synthesize the information as homework, to be turned in at the next class.

Evaluation/ Assessment:

Students will be evaluated on their level of participation in class discussions, quality of responses to discussion questions, their papers, and the content and delivery of their presentations.

Vocabulary:

symbolism, culture, Hip Hop, folktale, preserve, values, entertainment, metaphor, plague, pillage, quest, malicious, oblige, band, fortress, retrieve, triumph, prosperity, conquest, surpass

Extension Activities:

1. Have students brainstorm or suggest story topics based on their experiences with this class activity or in the past with their families. Discuss how these stories are the same and different from the ones groups shared. This can be done as a writing assignment or as a closing activity to this lesson.

2. Students can share family experiences with telling folktales as a means of educating children and teaching valuable life lessons. This can be done in an essay format which can be presented to the class during the next class meeting.

3. Have students listen to "Children's Story" by Slick Rick, a classic Hip Hop folktale, and investigate further how values and cultural experience inform even popular forms of art and music.

4. Have students read one of the following Japanese folktales for homework. Students must read the English versions and write a 1-2 page essay illustrating the use of metaphor and symbolism.

Bryan, Ashley. *Sh-ko and His Eight Wicked Brothers.* New York: Atheneum, 1988.

McDermott, Gerald. *The Stonecutter.* New York: Viking, 1975.

Snyder, Dianne. *The Boy of the Three-Year Nap.* Boston: Houghton, 1988.

Tejima, Keizaburo. *Ho-Limlim: A Rabbit Tale from Japan.* New York: Philomel, 1988.

Uchida, Yoshiko. *The Two Foolish Cats.* New York: Macmillan, 1987.

Other Information on the Web

Japanese Cultural Links on the World-Wide Web
http://www.ouc.bc.ca/arts/mola/jp/links-culture.htm

Japan Information
http://SunSITE.sut.ac.jp/asia/japan

Hip Hop Japan

http://www.hiphopjapan.com/

History of Hip Hop Dance in Japan

http://www.msu.edu/user/okumurak/japan/history.html

"Japan grows its own hip hop," BBC News, 1/17/2003

http://news.bbc.co.uk/2/hi/asia-pacific/3324409.stm

Interdisciplinary Connections:

Geography- Where in the world is Hip Hop Culture today? Research rappers, graffiti writers, b-boys/girls (break-dancers), or DJs on other continents and create an illustrated world map including artists from as many different countries as you can. Extend your list by including American Hip Hop artists of various ethnicities and identifying their countries of origin.

Global Studies- Research a Hip Hop artist in or from another country. Identify a piece of the artist's work that reflects the traditional values of their culture and prepare a presentation for the class which presents the artist, the work, and tells how it reflects the ethnic traditions of that particular culture.

Creative Writing- Write your own retelling of Momotaro that reflects your own personal values and beliefs. How is your Momotaro born? What does Momotaro's mother give him instead of dumplings? What animals do Momotaro encounter on his journey and how do they help in

battle? Who are the demons in your story and how do they plague the village? Write an essay explaining how your story is different from the original version and why.

"Maramoto" by Real Talk

Introduction

A long, long time ago- a child born from the fruit of nothingness/

Strong, growing rapidly - willing to do anything for his struggling family/

Even slay demons- So on a journey to go see them/

the child set and met three animals to help defeat them,

and the first you will meet is…

Verse One- The Dog

It's your dog, what you got? Food for thought, on your belt,

and that mic that I smelled/ I felt that you may need a companion,

I'll have your back like wherever you're standing, I'm with you,

In traveling, your best friend!

Nasty dog, cosmic dog,

Atomic, allotropic dog and I rocks it dog/

Demons take a look at my chompers and its problem solved/

I'll *pull up the flank*, take 'em from the back, they can't want none of that- aye,

What is it? Feed me right, I need a mic to speak my life, day leads to night/

Safety you will find in a straight piece of mind - I won't stray,

One trick I know, 'Stay!' and its all day, it's a long way/

Don't rub me the wrong way, my hearing is impeccable,

Mamma was a wolf, and Daddy was a boxer, fading any biter or barker/

74

I don't take crap, and I want paid naps,

Let's keep it moving, look here comes another cat·

Verse Two- The Monkey

Uhkiki monki ki they call me D the monkey/

I'm so hungry, but I ain't got no money/

Seems like demons took all the food from the hood, in the woods/

Somebody got to change it for the good of it/

Motivate people to see the truth of the system/

Slay them demons, nobody going to miss them/

Everybody got to get together and think what to do/

To change this thing, we need to form a crew like Wu

So unite in the name of the MOMOTARO/

And let it go, the hatred and the greed, to the cash and dough/

Check it, every negativity, is a possibility, to the positivity/

Admit it, so the demons, the system just- eat them like banana split/

Smoke them, but not cannabis, and focus so you see the mess/

I got my mic, so let's start the journey/

Open the map, oh wait yo- here comes another cat/

Verse Three- The Bird

The story unfolds as I peruse the nest cold/

From the swarm be the warm migration I'm pacing/

To daybreak and awaiting this change of landscaping/ (scenery)

Drawn to a group of land-walkers traveling/

A figure named Momotaro began unraveling the story of demons battling/

I asked him what he got, for food for thought, and a mic on his belt,

on a mission to hell/

To return balance to the universe is what he had felt/

And so I helped/ we set forth on a quest for freedom/

Hot on the trail of these corporate celestial beings/

Searching far and wide, I glide beyond the skies and see the isles of the demons/

I swoop to see 'em/

Started gaging the gatekeeper's eyes out bloody/

Motioning the crew to move before the guards come running/

Monkeys swings down to the ground and takes some heads out/

Dogs snivels with anger with chunks of meat and skin out/

The demon spirit flees as the overlord Oni cackles/

Emerging from the darkness Momotaro engaged in battle/

A test of will, the strength of a golden child prevails/

The corporate Mogol flails and retreats into the caverns entrails/

The champions rejoice with a victory beyond words/

And the group relished with the infinite treasures for living the message of change/

And the essence of where they came was for the love of the Hip Hop/

for the pain/ for the blame/

D. "Khazm" Kogita (For Real Talk Copyright 2005)

The Legend of Momotaro

Adaptation by Daichi Sawa and Julie Chang Schulman

A long, long time ago, in a plagued Japanese village, there lived an old man and his wife. One day, when the old man was in the mountains cutting wood, his wife went to wash clothes down at the river. As she was washing, she was surprised to see a huge peach floating down the river. She quickly picked it up.

When she got home with the big peach, she presented it to her surprised husband, who decided it would make a good meal. Just as the old man went to chop the peach in half, the couple heard a small voice from inside! Carefully, the old man split the fruit open, and they were delighted to find nestled within it, a new baby boy. They decided to call him Momotaro, the Peach Boy, and raised him as their own. As the years went by, Momotaro grew so fast and strong that by the time he was fifteen, he had already surpassed the strength of many adults in his village.

One day, the brave Momotaro announced that he was departing for Demon Island on a journey to rid the village of its suffering forever. The demons of the island were malicious and greedy monsters that terrorized the people and pillaged the land for all its food and treasure. As Momotaro set out on his quest, his old mother gave him three kibidango (sweet dumplings) for his journey, which he tied on his belt. Soon, a dog approached Momotaro and sang a song, offering his companionship and help in exchange for a dumpling. Momotaro obliged, and as the duo traveled, a monkey approached with the same song and offer, to which Momotaro obliged. As the three made their way toward Demon Island, a bird approached singing the song, and Momotaro once again accepted the offer.

When the band arrived at Demon Island, the bird flew over the walls, retrieved the key, and opened the gate to the Demons' fortress for the other three. As they entered and began to battle, the bird pecked the eyes of the demons and their leader Oni, the dog bit their legs, and the monkey clawed their backs until the evil monsters cried out for mercy! Conquered, they gave brave Momotaro all the treasures they had stolen, and the boy returned to his village triumphantly, bringing peace and prosperity to all the land.

Lesson 2: Identifying and Utilizing Visual Language in Poetry/Narrative Writing

Author(s): Sarah Montgomery-Glinski

Bio: Sarah Montgomery-Glinski was born in Boston, Massachusetts. She has studied education policy and urban education at New York University and attained a Masters in Special Education at Mercy College through New York City Teaching Fellows. She has taught at the elementary, middle and high school levels, working with general and special needs populations. Sarah is currently teaching at the High School for Art and Technology.

Grades: 7-9   **Subjects:** Language Arts

Academic Content Standards: Language Arts Standard 1- Demonstrates competence in the general skills and strategies of the writing process. Language Arts Standard 7- Demonstrates competence in the general skills and strategies for reading a variety of informational texts. Music Standard 7- Understands the relationship between music and history and culture.

Overview of Lesson Plan: In this lesson, students will analyze Tupac's *The Case of the Missing Mic* in terms of voice, detail and sequence in order to create a rubric and become more conscious of those elements in their own writing.

Suggested Time Allowance: One Hour

Objectives: Students will analyze the concept of moral or lesson through Tupac's *Case of the Missing Mic* connecting it to an upcoming assignment to write a personal narrative highlighting an experience where they overcame a challenge or dealt with personal failure. Students will combine their knowledge of prior examples personal narratives, (memoirs, biographies, etc.) as a class and have a clear understanding of the flexibility of style (voice, format) allowed for their personal narrative, as well as the detail necessary by creating a rubric for the personal narrative assignment.

Resources/Materials:

-Song Lyrics (www.ohhla.com)

-Pens, paper , chart paper

-Overhead Projector (Optional)

-CD player

-Copy of *The Case of the Missing Mic* (www.ohhla.com)

-Rubric worksheet

78

Activities/Procedures:

Warm-Up:

Students receive lyrics and a prompt to create a rubric highlighting the important aspects of a personal narrative focused on overcoming a challenge or personal failure. Students work in pairs or threes to complete the worksheet and are prompted to skim over the lyrics as an example of this kind of narrative.

Before discussing the rubrics, students listen to the song *The Case of the Missing Mic* by Tupac Shakur listening and comparing their rubrics to the lyrics/delivery of the song.

Work Period:

As a whole class, students discuss the merits of this song as compared to their rubrics. Pairs/trios are given chart paper to write responses they agree uphold the standards of the rubric they have developed. The strongest elements/standards are reaffirmed by the teacher who is simultaneously creating a rubric from the responses of students on an overhead projector.

Individual:

Students receive writing assignment: Create a rough draft of a personal narrative focusing on the elements outlined on the rubric on the overhead projector. Students work individually to begin their narratives.

Closing:

Students are prompted to read their work and discuss the similarities to Tupac's *The Case of the Missing Mic*, as well as how they plan on developing their work in the framework of the rubric.

Further Questions for Discussion:

-Why might we use an example of a personal narrative before writing our own?

-Why would this example assist us in understanding the criteria for the assignment?

-Does using this example limit or expand the writing styles you might use when completing the assignment?

Evaluation/Assessment:

Students will be evaluated based on how closely their rough drafts fulfill the criteria of the assignment as determined by the class-constructed rubric.

Lesson 3: The Story I RIGHT: Hip-Hop & Personal Narrative Writing

Author(s): Unique Fraser

Bio: Unique has a strong background with NYC after-school programs serving public high school students. As an educator, she is committed to academic excellence as well as creating rigorous and positive learning environments. Unique is a native and current resident of Brooklyn, New York.

Grades: 9-12   **Subjects:** College Planning; English; Language Arts; Creative Writing

Academic Content Standards: Language Arts Standard 1- Demonstrates competence in the general skills and strategies of the writing process. Language Arts Standard 2- Demonstrates competence in the stylistic and rhetorical aspects of writing. Language Arts Standard 4- Gathers and uses information for research purposes. Language Arts Standard 7- Demonstrates competence in the general skills and strategies for reading a variety of informational texts. Music Standard 7- Understands the relationship between music and history and culture.

Overview of the Lesson Plan: "The Story I RIGHT" is a personal narrative writing lesson that uses elements of hip-hop to help students identify new and creative ways of talking about themselves critically for the personal statement of their college applications. The goals of this project are to introduce students to other forms of narrative writing—*particularly storytelling*—in hip hop to understand the ways that other narrators tell stories about the world around them. Personal storytelling is a critical way for a young person to communicate their ideas, feelings, politics—*their stories*—in their own words, on their own terms, for the college essay and otherwise. Oftentimes the stories that our young people tell paint a reality that is largely different from the ones that are in the media. By telling their own stories, students ultimately begin to re-write or RIGHT the stories that have been created for them. Students also build a foundation of personal narrative writing that will help them be successful for the college classroom and beyond. In this lesson, students will examine the lyrics to "The Message" by Grandmaster Flash.

Suggested Time: One hour

Objectives:

- Introduce students to the genres of **narrative** and **storytelling**

- Have students think critically about **hip-hop music lyrics** as an **important learning tool** for **critical thinking** and **narrative writing**

- Prepare students to **write their own personal narrative** (for the college essay)

Resources / Materials:

- Chalk board/dry erase board

- Paper

- Pen/pencil

- Copies of music lyrics for each student

- CD player & a copy of Grandmaster Flash's "The Message"

Activities/Procedures:

A. Discussion: How are STORIES told? (15 minutes)

- Before students enter the classroom, the instructor should write the terms "narrative" and "storytelling" on the board

- Once students have settled in and taken out a piece of paper and a pen, the instructor should lead a discussion where students define "narrative" and "storytelling"

- The instructor should encourage students to call out ideas and definitions that come to mind when they think of these terms; the instructor should generate a list of definitions on the board based on student responses

- Once students have generated a substantive list, the instructor should encourage further discussion about the role of narrative and storytelling in their personal lives. Consider the following questions:

  -What kinds of stories does our society tell of young people?

  -Do the stories differ based on race and class?

  -Where do these images and perspectives come from?

  -How are students critical of these perspectives?

  -What are the critiques of these perspectives?

  -Is there anything about these stories that needs to change?

- Instructor should write down student responses as they are being generated

B. Discussion: Quick Mix Theories OR Social Commentaries? (30 minutes)

- Once students have generated a list of ideas about how stories are told by the media and

society, the instructor should transition the discussion into hip-hop as storytelling

- Instructor should ask the students the following questions:

    -What kinds of stories are told in hip-hop?

    -Who are the stories about?

    -What critiques does hip-hop offer about society?

- Instructor should then distribute copies of Grandmaster Flash's, "The Message", to each student

- The instructor should briefly explain who Grandmaster Flash is, discuss his contribution to hip-hop as a DJ (his pioneering approach of 'scratching' or 'quick mixing'), as a rapper, discuss when the song was written and where the story takes place (early 1980's, New York City)

- Students should volunteer to read the lyrics out loud and talk about each line

- As students are reading the lyrics out loud, the instructor should help students critically discuss the "story" that Grandmaster Flash is telling. Questions to consider:

    -What is the story that is being told by Grandmaster Flash?

    -Why is the song entitled, "The Message"?

    -What critique(s) is the artist making?

    -Who is the audience?

    -Are there any perceptions of society that the artist is trying to challenge or make "right"?

- Once students have read through the lyrics of the song, the instructor should play the song on CD player

3. Discussion: Students Identify their Favorite Hip Hop Lyrics (10 minutes)

    - The instructor should generate a discussion with students about their favorite artists and the kinds of stories that are being told

    - Students are encouraged to think about how the stories they identify from their

favorite artists are similar to or different from Grandmaster Flash's story

D. Homework Assignment (5 minutes)

- Students should examine the lyrics of their favorite hip-hop song and write a one-page free write critiquing the story that is being told

Additional Narrative Writing Approaches:

1. Graffiti: Public Lives, Visual Stories

- Students can examine graffiti as a means of public story telling

- Show the documentary, "Style Wars"

- Display and discuss photographs from Hunts Point, Queens; do walking tours of the city and document graffiti

2. Photography: Shifting the GAZE, Adjusting the LENS

- Students can examine photography and the work of pre-selected photographers to think about how visual imagery tells different stories from varied perspectives

- Students can be challenged to think about the difference in how stories are told when it's a visual story (i.e., a photograph) or a written story (i.e., music lyrics, graffiti writing, fiction writing, etc.)

College Board New SAT: http://www.collegeboard.com/about/news_info/sat/index.html

Lesson 4: Title: Listen and Write Activity

Author(s): Andrew Landers

Bio: Andrew Landers owes unlimited gratitude to his brothers for, among other things, the influence of Hip-Hop on his life. Co-Leader of the Hip-Hop Association's Education Committee, A. holds a Masters Degree in Literacy from The City College of New York and graduated from Boston University's School of Education. Now with five years experience teaching students with special needs in NYC public schools, A. has been an educator since 1995.

Grades: 6-8, 9-12   **Subject Areas**: Language Arts

Overview of Lesson Plan: The Listen and Write is an activity developed by A Landers designed to improve student ability to access language, form sentences, and build vocabulary. After studying specific word types, students are given the opportunity to access that knowledge and practice word retrieval skills. The activity can be applied to any relevant text by analyzing the text, selecting appropriate words to omit, and developing questions that will activate multiple areas of brain functioning. Hip-Hop and Hip-Hop related topics are a good source for these activities and stimulate interest, knowledge, and discussion.

Academic Content Standards: Language Arts Standard 1- Demonstrates competence in the general skills and strategies of the writing process. Language Arts Standard 2- Demonstrates competence in the stylistic and rhetorical aspects of writing. Language Arts Standard 4- Gathers and uses information for research purposes. Language Arts Standard 7- Demonstrates competence in the general skills and strategies for reading a variety of informational texts. Music Standard 7- Understands the relationship between music and history and culture.

Materials:

- Copy of article or book selection. (attached)

- Listen and write worksheet. (attached)

Procedure:

1. Begin by reading instructions together and checking that they are understood. If a particular type of word is requested (noun, verb, adjective), discuss definition and show examples.

2. Ask a question to stimulate background knowledge about the subject.

   EX. Have you heard about Bill Cosby in the news lately? *Or* What are some of the criticisms you hear about hip-hop?

3. Read the beginning of the article or book selection, up to the point where students are asked to fill in the blanks.

4. Allow students time to read through the paragraph and enter appropriate words. Encourage them to reread their answers and ask themselves: Does this make sense?

5. Student volunteers can read their paragraphs with substitutions, generating a discussion on whether or not they make sense.

6. Read the *actual* paragraph from the article and continue to the end.

7. Allow students time to read and respond to questions.

8. Discuss. The following reading selection was taken from, <u>Is Bill Cosby Right? Or has the black middle class lost its mind?</u>, by Michael Eric Dyson, pg. 9, Basic Civitas Books.

Cosby's comments betray the ugly generational divide in black America. His disregard for the hip-hop generation is not unique, but it still disheartening. Cosby's poisonous view of young folk who speak a language he can barely parse simmers with hostility and resentment. And yet, some of the engaged critique he seeks to make of black folk- of their materialism, their consumptive desires, their personal choices, their moral aspirations, their social conscience- is broadcast with much more imagination and insight in certain quarters of hip-hop culture. (Think Kanye West's track, "All Falls Down", which displays a self-critical approach to the link between consumption and the effort to ward of racial degradation.) Cosby detests youth for their hip-hop dress, body-piercing and the pseudo-African-sounding names they have. Yet, body piercing and baggy clothes express identity among black youth, and not just beginning hip-hop culture. Moreover, young black entrepreneurs like Sean "P. Diddy" Combs and Russell Simmons have made millions from their clothing lines. There are generational tensions over self-definition; arguments over clothes and body markings reflect class, age and intracultural conflicts as well.

Listening & Writing

This is an excerpt taken from Michael Eric Dyson's <u>Is Bill Cosby Right</u>?, pg. 9. After listening to part of the text read to you by your teacher, complete the sentences (*with nouns*) to make an interesting and sensible paragraph.

     Cosby detests _____ for their hip-hop dress, body piercing and the

pseudo-African-sounding _____ they have. Yet, body piercing and baggy

_____ express identity among black youth, and not just beginning with hip-hop

_____. Moreover, young black _____ like Sean "P. Diddy"

Combs and Russell Simmons have made _____ from their clothing lines. There are

generational _____ over self-definition; arguments over clothes and body

markings reflect class, age and intracultural conflicts as well.

When you are done, wait for your teacher to read the conclusion of the selection.

Answer the following questions:

1. What are two of Cosby's arguments against black youth in America?

2. Give an example from your own life experience and observation of what Dyson calls "generational tensions over self-definition".

3. Dyson uses Kanye West's "All Falls Down" as an example of an insightful critique of black America. Write your own insightful critique of a problem you think faces *your* people, *your* society, or *your* culture. What is the problem, what causes it, and what should be done?

Lesson 5: Poetry Rap-Up: Finding Literary Devices and Themes in Lyrics

Author(s): Ellen Warkentine

Bio: Ellen Warkentine is a first year fifth grade teacher with a passion for poetry and the performing arts. She is currently teaching in South Los Angeles and is working towards her M.Ed in the social-justice oriented Teacher Education Program at UCLA.

Grades: 6-8, 9-12   **Subject Area:** Language Arts

Objectives:

- Students will analyze poetry in the lyrics of a Hip-Hop song, identifying and explaining the use of literary devices within the song, including rhyme, assonance, alliteration, imagery, metaphor, symbolism and figures of speech.

- Students will discuss poetry and write about it in journals

- Students will write at least one stanza (a few lines) of a poem/rap based on a theme or big idea we are studying in social studies, science, or language arts. Theme may also be personal if approved by the teacher.

- Students will perform the lines for the class to the rhythm of beat-boxing or in the form of a poem.

Academic Content Standards: Language Arts Standard 1- Demonstrates competence in the general skills and strategies of the writing process. Language Arts Standard 2- Demonstrates competence in the stylistic and rhetorical aspects of writing. Language Arts Standard 4- Gathers and uses information for research purposes. Language Arts Standard 7- Demonstrates competence in the general skills and strategies for reading a variety of informational texts. Music Standard 7- Understands the relationship between music and history and culture.

Resources / Materials:

- "Alphabet Aerobics" by Blackalicious (language play) (www.ohhla.com)

- "Hard Times" by Run DMC (social issues/the world) (www.ohhla.com)

- "Africa Dream" by Talib Kweli lyrics (social issues/entertainment critique) (www.ohhla.com)

- MP3/CD player

- Scavenger Hunt/Lyrics Packet

- Lyrics transparencies

Assessments:

- Students will be assessed formally through what they write in their lyrics packets, in terms of identifying literary devices from the scavenger hunt where they appear in the songs.

- Students will be assessed in their journal responses to the free response question, on whether or not they put thought into the answers to the focus questions.

- Students will be assessed informally through observations during group work.

- Students will be assessed in the rap they write according to the criteria that the rap must include at least 3 literary devices from the list and must relate to a theme we are studying in class or personal theme if approved by the teacher.

Instructional Strategies and Learning Tasks to Support Student Learning

- Teacher will begin class by playing "Alphabet Aerobics" by Blackalicious. Instructions will be on the board to have students quietly get out journals and respond to the following focus questions: "Is rap poetry? Is all rap poetry? What does it take for something to be considered 'poetry'?" Students will take a position and begin class by writing down in their journals free responses to these questions. They will be reminded that "there is no right answer" to these questions. After they write for 5 minutes, Students will pair-share their answers in a 5-minute discussion and then share out to the class.

- Teacher will hand out a "Scavenger Hunt" packet to the students. The packet will include lyrics to "Alphabet Aerobics" by Blackalicious, "Hard Times," by Run DMC, and "Africa Dream," by Talib Kweli. On the front page of the packet, there is a list of literary devices, including the following terms:

  - Imagery

  - Figures of speech

  - Simile

  - Metaphor

  - Alliteration or Assonance

- Onomatopoeia

- Symbolism

- Hyperbole

- Rhyme

- Theme

- Teacher will model the search for the terms in the lyrics of "Alphabet Aerobics," reviewing each term as they search for the literary devices. Teacher will review the meaning of "literary device" and discuss how poets use devices to make language more colorful, and to bring images and ideas to life. Going over each term, the teacher will ask students to try and circle any of those things they find in "Alphabet Aerobics," going down the list and asking questions.

- Students will follow/rap along with the next song, "Hard Times," by Run DMC. After the class listens to the first song together, the teacher will give students 10 minutes to analyze the rap in their sections/groups, and also to write what they think the "theme" of the song is. Students will share out after 10 minutes.

- Teacher will call students' attention to the complex lyrics of "Africa Dream," and the class will work together to analyze the final rap. Teacher will lead discussion on the meanings of rap, Hip-Hop, and poetry, started by the guiding question based on Kweli's and Blackalicious' ideas about other rappers and why they are criticizing the kind of rap on the radio. Revisit journals for this discussion, ask students to write down any new thoughts from the second discussion after analysis.

- Students will begin group work on writing their own rap song. Students must include at least 3 literary devices from the list. Students will work the rest of the lesson to complete the rap, and the students who finish will perform. Some students may have to perform the next day due to time limits.

Accommodations or additional support to meet student needs in instruction and assessment

- Students will be working in flexible groups with a variety of students at different instructional levels, and there will be many opportunities for the teacher and peers to scaffold the scavenger hunt activity for students with special needs.

- Students will respond to the rhythms and familiar music in the poetry and rhyme of the rap songs, allowing students a chance to choral read rhythmically.

- Teacher will allow students time for personal reflections, giving students many spaces in class to reflect where there are no "right" answers, in a safe space.

- Clear printed lyrics and large overhead.

Theory:

This lesson plan is informed by sociocultural theory as a whole, as students are creating knowledge and working with peers in learning communities. Specifically, this theory is informed by the language theory ideas of H. Samy Alim. In his article, "Black Language in White Public Space," Alim discusses the language practices involved in Hip-Hop culture and the verbal art of rhyming. In this lesson, students are given a space in class where the language practices of Hip-Hop are valued, and students are asked identify the same literary elements in rap that are found in traditional poetry, thereby demonstrating that the Hip-Hop vernacular and Standard English both share essential features, and in this case Standard English is not the privileged form. According to Alim, there is a notion of "linguistic supremacy" in schools according to white norms, where Standard English is privileged. In this lesson, non-standard English is emphasized as a place of power and expression, which furthers Alim's cause of working towards "linguistic equanimity."

Background Information: I chose to create a lesson plan that allows students to really think about the language involved in their cultural practice; this lesson gives students a chance to discuss the importance of Hip-Hop lyrics with peers. A lot of the students in my student teaching placement who were involved in this cultural practice did not think of the lyrics as important, and some said they "just listened to the music" or the beat of a rap song. The lesson plan emphasizes the language and poetry of rap, valuing the ways ideas are expressed in three different rap songs, each with different themes and a variety of literary devices. I used Alim's theory of linguistic supremacy and equanimity to create my lessons. Though in the lesson the class is still talking about a form of non-standard English in terms This of Standard English, it is not necessarily comparing and contrasting rap and other poetry- it is valuing the genre on its own as an equally legitimate form of expression. Students also get an opportunity to use their own language to create a rap. The only requirements are that the students use 3 literary devices, but it is up to them how "standard" the English is. This is also important, according to Alim, and I thought of his lecture on creating spaces for non-standard English in the classroom. This is a lesson that does just that, by presenting students with non-standard English in a way that values the art form of Hip-Hop, and it also gives students an opportunity to express through personal, non-standard forms of English.

More Information on Academic Standards: Reading 3.1. Identify and analyze the characteristics of poetry, drama, fiction, and nonfiction and explain the appropriateness of the literary forms chosen by an author for a specific purpose. Reading 3.4. Understand that *theme* refers to the meaning or moral of a selection and recognize themes (whether implied or stated directly) in sample works. Reading 3.5 Describe the function and effect of common literary devices (e.g., imagery, metaphor, symbolism). Listening and Speaking 1.9 Read prose and poetry aloud with fluency, rhythm, and pace, using appropriate intonation and vocal patterns to emphasize important passages of the text being read.

II. HISORY, GLOBAL STUDIES AND GEOGRAPHY

Hip-Hop culture is a worldwide movement that is important to our collective, shared knowledge of history and culture. These lessons reflect on the significance of the movement in a global and historical context.

Albanian - Algerian - American - Angolan - Arabic - Asian - Australian - Austrian - Azerbaijani - Bahraini - Belgian - Bosnian and Herzegovinan - Botswana - Brazilian - British - Bulgarian - Canadian - Cape Verdean - Chinese - Congolese - Cuban - Czech - Danish - Dominican - Dutch - Egyptian - European - Filipino - Finnish - French - Gambian - German - Ghanaian - Greek - Greenlandic - Guinean - Hong Kong - Hungarian - Icelandic - Indian - Indonesian - Irish - Israeli - Italian - Ivoirian - Japanese - Kenyan - Korean - Latin American - Lebanese - Malagasy - Malaysian - Malian - Mexican - Moroccan - Native American - Nepalese - New Zealand - Nigerian - Nigerien - Norwegian - Polish - Portuguese - Puerto Rican - Romanian - Russian - Rwandan - Salvadoran - Senegalese - Serbian - Singaporean - Slovak - Slovenian - Somali - South African - Spanish - Swedish - Swiss - Taiwanese - Tanzanian - Togolese - Turkish - Ugandan - Ukrainian - Zimbabwean

- **Lesson 1: Self-Hate: Implication Towards Assimilation**

  Author(s): Charan Morris

- **Lesson 2: International Hip-Hop Geography**

  Author(s): Daniel Zarazua

- **Lesson 3: What Prophet?**

  Author(s): Andrew Landers

These are just some of the recognized hip-hop movements around the world.

-Wikipedia.org

Worldhiohop

- **Lesson 4: *Who Am I?* Using DNA to Determine Ancestry Cultural Identity**

  Author(s): Gina Paige

93

Lesson 1: Self-Hate: Implications Towards Assimilation

Note: Due to the subject of this lesson, the author has chosen to use the N-Word as part of the dialogue on racism and internalized oppression.

Author(s): Charan Morris

Bio: Charan Morris is an experienced educator, hailing from Chicago. She attended New York University, and is currently teacher in the New York City public school system.

Grades: 6-8, 9-12   **Subject Areas**: American History, Language Arts, Social Studies

Academic Content Standards: Language Arts Standard 1- Demonstrates competence in the general skills and strategies of the writing process. Language Arts Standard 2- Demonstrates competence in the stylistic and rhetorical aspects of writing. Language Arts Standard 4- Gathers and uses information for research purposes. Language Arts Standard 7- Demonstrates competence in the general skills and strategies for reading a variety of informational texts. Music Standard 7- Understands the relationship between music and history and culture. Language Arts Standard 8- Demonstrates competence in speaking and listening as tools for learning. United States History Standard 31- Understands economic, social, and cultural developments in the contemporary United States. Behavioral Studies Standard 2- Understands various meanings of social group, general implications of group membership, and different ways that groups function.

Overview of Lesson Plan: Students will begin to understand the origin of self-hate (internalized oppression) for African-Americans and other oppressed groups.

Suggested Time Allowance: One hour

Resources / Materials:

Pictures of black caricatures (from Jim Crow memorabilia website):
http://www.ferris.edu/jimcrow/menu.htm

Song and Lyrics of Goodie Mob's "Nigga" (lyrics included) (www.ohhla.com)

Activities / Procedures:

Motivation (2 parts):

Pictures of black caricatures (from Jim Crow memorabilia website):

How do these images make black people look? If these were the only images of people that are

you race that you ever saw, what would you begin to think about yourself?

Students will listen to the following song and answer the following Questions:

Goodie Mob's Song: "Nigga"

- What does Cee-Lo say makes someone a nigga? What does he say does not make someone a nigga?

- What do you think Cee-Lo thinks of people who call themselves niggas? What is Cee-Lo trying to say about the use of the word Nigga in this song?

Motivation Discussion:

Students will share their responses to both medias (song and caricatures):

Are these two things (song and caricatures) related in any way? How do you think they are related?

Mini Lesson:

What is self-hatred (often caused by external forces)? What are the reasons for self-hatred? What is American society's idea of beautiful?

Brief history of what led to black people's self-hatred and brief history of the origin of the N-word:

- Internalization of negative images of ourselves in the 1800s. Images became accepted as truth?

Homework:

Response Paper (choose one of the two)

How does self-hatred relate to assimilation for African-Americans? Does the existence of self-hatred amongst a minority group become a reason for assimilation? If so is the assimilation voluntary or involuntary?

OR

Is the existence of negative images such as caricatures that cause self-hatred within a society cause human suffering? Can human suffering propel a person/people to assimilate?

Evaluation / Assessment:

Student participation, evaluation of paper

Extension Activities 1:

Read lyrics to song

Read Mos Def's Speech "Assata Shakur: The government's terrorist is our community's heroine" (www.ohhla.com) attached

Discuss: As a class, talk about what more we want to learn about Assata Shakur. These two contemporary figures in Hip-Hop felt the need to addressing her life through the song Common Sense and through Mos Def's speech.

- Why do these two contemporary figures in Hip-Hop feel it is significant to be speaking about Shakur?

- Why would it be important to know about her for your own lives?

Extension Activities 2:

Read Assata: An Autobiography and discuss:

Why did putting the word black behind every insult make the insult worse?

What does this tell us about what it meant to be black for Assata growing up?

Where do you think they got this meaning from?

Was this meaning at all related to stereotypes about being black?

Why does she think black is ugly? Where did she get this opinion?

Where do you think Assata got the idea that being dark skinned in ugly?

Does this type of thinking about skin color amongst black people still exist?

How do these excerpts relate to Cee-Lo's commentary on black people's use of the word nigga?

How do these excerpts relate to the affect that the caricatures had on black people?

Lyrics: Goodie Mob "Good Nigga"

[Big Gipp]
We fixin' run this shit
We fixin' to put our own shit out

[Verse 1: Big Gipp]
From A-Town, so I'ma put up my hood
You pay for what chu' get, determines whether you chief ridin'
Live, keep good
If a job don't find you, struggle usually will
Mostly attracted at this skill, makin' you feel
Ugly inside, huh, and the feel pretty about my lifestyle
Cause I get mine, apartment complex and services since I was a child
So it ain't shit for me to clamp down on my hearts
Uh, try Mr. Ed, throwin' bow in the middle where niggas don't dance
All they do is scrap
I signed the club and back of niggas trucks
Master told ya how it get, I sell more drug fire
Run away slave and challenges growin' up
Ya shit's shaved and bathed
Hit the stage and split it four ways
Then after they end up in state
You be so raged like you can't really get Scarface
Rap-A-Lot slashed away
But don't be too star struck to realize
What's being done to you on a regular basis
Plus it's never been education
Still workin' for the white man
Still got em' pissed off in this custom
Shave yo head, trim yo bill
And don't forget to get real
Watch you grill, some wounds never heal
So we erasin' motivated hate crimes

[Chorus: Cee-Lo]
Yeah, well I'm a truth nigga
Not a brand new nigga
A do what I gotta do nigga
A just like you nigga
A just tryin' to make it through nigga
Like I should nigga, hood nigga
I'm a good nigga
Yeah, well I'm a truth nigga
Not a brand new nigga

A do what I gotta do nigga
A just like you nigga
A just tryin' to make it through nigga
Like I should nigga, hood nigga
I'm a good nigga

[Verse 2: Khujo]
It's the A-Town slum all up in the mic
Need to ride the Converse, switch it up with the Nike
Smokin' Wayne reds and them o-r blunts
Candy apple Lac with the rght on the trunk
Somewhere, some fell man soft and hard
Always would chase paper to stop my heart
Wasn't on anything that ain't me, trust this
To my cousin, set free I'ma drop this
I got shit that'll go through walls
And when I click, it ain't no laws
We get buck, crunk from here to Houston
Rockin' straw hats, drinkin' outta big jars
Swirvin' into big ships scopin' out the next way to get paid
Gotta a phone call from Lil' J

[Cee-Lo & Khujo]
OK we on the way y'all (OK we on the way homeboy)
OK we on the way y'all (OK we on the way homeboy)

[Chorus]

[Verse 3: Cee-Lo]
Well I don't wanna take too much of ya time
But cha' now how I get when I start to rhyme
Come on, something gets in him and he starts talking the talk
Get up in yo mind and provokin' the thought
OK I teach the day, yesterday for the day we died
Everyday like everything is OK
They good, they down for they pride, they down for they side
They down for they ride, they always try, they die
Niggas ain't real when they rappin'
So I put my crackin' to casual cappin'
Statistics waitin' to happen
Oh, and let me tell ya what's next
I'm used to braggin' macho, be gettin' Rolex
They gonna take ya baby mama welfare check
Cause I'ma for real, up in the projects
And what they say, realize the blow

Shake that thang cause you can't make money no mo'
We searchin' but we ain't got no strategies that fold
Ya gon' lose when the pack is on roll, for sho'
Oh and it's on but do what cha' what cha' want
I just want it to be known, and I'm gone
F****in' with the 5th Ward and the 4th it's on

[Chorus]

[Verse 4: T-Mo]
Misunderstood is a good nigga goin' un-reported
Coke be goin' sold next homicides, drive by's (Da, da, da)
At my spot, at the angel spot so hot
That we don't even see y'all passin' us by
Leavin' although we exhibit the pain
So much pain for a young, ready to gun nigga
Watch out for the day, thinkin' bout the
Dirty past, with the future bout to bust you in ya face
You didn't know that Ghetto Boys and Goodie Mob was in the place
We workin' on a punk ass nigga
That thought this motherf*****' shit was flirt
Bad niggas work and I'ma work
And give me love when we hit the scene
Ya know what I mean

[Chorus]

Assata Shakur: The government's terrorist is our community's heroine

by Mos Def

Early in May, the federal government issued a statement in which they labeled Joanne Chesimard, known to most in the Black community as Assata Shakur, as a domestic terrorist. In so doing, they also increased the bounty on her head from $150,000 to an unprecedented $1,000,000.

Viewed through the lens of U.S. law enforcement, Shakur is an escaped cop-killer. Viewed through the lens of many Black people, including me, she is a wrongly convicted woman and a hero of epic proportions.

My first memory of Assata Shakur was the "Wanted" posters all over my Brooklyn neighborhood. They said her name was Joanne Chesimard, that she was a killer, an escaped convict, and armed and dangerous.

They made her sound like a super-villain, like something out of a comic book. But even then, as a child, I couldn't believe what I was being told.

When I looked at those posters and the mug shot of a slight, brown, high-cheekboned woman with a full afro, I saw someone who looked like she was in my family, an aunt, a mother.

She looked like she had soul. Later, as a junior high school student, when I read her autobiography, "Assata," I would discover that not only did she have soul, she also had immeasurable heart, courage and love.

And I would come to believe that that very heart and soul she possessed was exactly why Assata Shakur was shot, arrested, framed and convicted of the murder of a New Jersey State Trooper.

There are some undisputed facts about the case. On May 2, 1973, Assata Shakur, a Black Panther, was driving down the New Jersey State Turnpike with two companions, Zayd Shakur and Sundiata Acoli.

The three were pulled over, ostensibly for a broken tail light. A gun battle ensued; why and how it started is unclear. But the aftermath is not. Trooper Werner Forester and Zayd Shakur lay dead.

Sundiata Acoli escaped (he was captured two days later). And Assata was shot and arrested. At trial, three neurologists would testify that the first gunshot shattered her clavicle and the second shattered the median nerve in her right hand. That testimony proved that she was sitting with her hands raised when she was fired on by police.

Further testimony proved that no gun residue was found on either of her hands, nor were her fingerprints found on any of the weapons located at the scene. Nevertheless, Shakur was convicted by an all-White jury and sentenced to life in prison.

Six years and six months to the day that she was arrested, and aided by friends, Shakur escaped from Clinton Women's Prison in New Jersey. As a high school student, I remember seeing

100

posters all around the Brooklyn community I lived in that read: "Assata Shakur is Welcome Here." In 1984, she surfaced in Cuba and was granted political asylum by Fidel Castro.

There are those who believe that being convicted of a crime makes you guilty. But that imposes an assumption of infallibility upon our criminal justice system.

When Assata Shakur was convicted of killing Werner Foerster, not only had the Black Panther Party been labeled by then FBI Director J. Edgar Hoover as "the greatest internal threat" to American security, but Assata herself had been thoroughly criminalized in the minds of the American public.

She'd been charged in six different crimes, ranging from attempted murder to bank robbery, and her acquittal or dismissal of the charges outright notwithstanding, to the average citizen, it seemed she must be guilty of something. And she was. She was guilty of calling for a shift in power in America and for racial and economic justice.

Included on a short list of the many people who have made that call and were either criminalized, terrorized, killed or blacklisted are Paul Robeson, Martin Luther King, Schwerner, Chaney and Goodman, Medgar Evers and Ida B. Wells.

Perhaps what is most insulting about the government's latest attack on Assata is that while they vigorously pursue her extradition, a few years ago using it as a bargaining chip for lifting the embargo itself, they have been decidedly lackadaisical in pursuing the extradition to Venezuela of an admitted terrorist, Florida resident Luis Posada Carriles. Carriles is likely responsible for blowing up a Cuban airline in 1976, an act which claimed the lives of some 73 innocent civilians.

For those of us who either remember the state of the union in the 1960s and 1970s or have studied it, when we consider Assata Shakur living under political asylum in Cuba, we believe that nation is exercising its political sovereignty and in no way harboring a terrorist.

Cubans sees Assata as I, and many others in my community do: as a woman who was and is persecuted for her political beliefs.

When the federal government raised the bounty on her head this May 2, one official declared that Assata was merely "120 pounds of money." For many of us in the Black community, she could never be so reduced. For many of us in the Black community, she was and remains, to use her own words, an "escaped slave," a heroine, not unlike Harriet Tubman.

Common Sense ft. Cee-Lo
A Song for Assata

(Common)
In the Spirit of God.
In the Spirit of the Ancestors.
In the Spirit of the Black Panthers.
In the Spirit of Assata Shakur.
We make this movement towards freedom
for all those who have been oppressed, and all those in the struggle.
Yeah. yo, check it-

There were lights and sirens, gunshots firin
Cover your eyes as I describe a scene so violent
Seemed like a bad dream, she laid in a blood puddle
Blood bubbled in her chest, cold air brushed against open flesh
No room to rest, pain consumed each breath
Shot twice wit her hands up
Police questioned but shot before she answered
One Panther lost his life, the other ran for his
Scandalous the police were as they kicked and beat her
Comprehension she was beyond, tryna hold on
to life. She thought she'd live with no arm
that's what it felt like, got to the hospital, eyes held tight
They moved her room to room-she could tell by the light
Handcuffed tight to the bed, through her skin it bit
Put guns to her head, every word she got hit
"Who shot the trooper?" they asked her
Put mace in her eyes, threatened to blast her
Her mind raced till things got still
Opened her eyes, realized she's next to her best friend who got killed
She got chills, they told her: that's where she would be next
Hurt mixed wit anger-survival was a reflex
They lied and denied visits from her lawyer
But she was buildin as they tried to destroy her
If it wasn't for this german nurse they woulda served her worse
I read this sister's story, knew that it deserved a verse
I wonder what would happen if that woulda been me?
All this shit so we could be free, so dig it, y'all.

(Cee-lo vocals)
I'm thinkin' of Assata, yes.
Listen to my Love, Assata, yes.
Your Power and Pride is beautiful.
May God bless your Soul.

(Common)
It seemed like the middle of the night when the law awakened her
Walkie-talkies cracklin, I see 'em when they takin her
Though she kinda knew,
What made the ride peaceful was the trees and the sky was blue
Arrived to Middlesex Prison about six inna morning
Uneasy as they pushed her to the second floor in
a cell, one cot, no window, facing hell.
Put in the basement of a prison wit all males
And the smell of misery, seatless toilets and centipedes
She'd exercise, (paint?,) and begin to read
Two years inna hole. Her soul grew weak
Away from people so long she forgot how to speak
She discovered frredom is a unspoken sound
And a wall is a wall and can be broken down
Found peace in the Panthers she went on trial with
One of the brothers she had a child with
The foulness they would feed her, hopin she's lose her seed
Held tight, knowing the fight would live through this seed
In need of a doctor, from her stomach she's bleed
Out of this situation a girl was conceived
Separated from her, left to mother the Revolution
And lactated to attack hate
Cause federal and state was built for a Black fate
Her emptiness was filled with beatings and court dates
They fabricated cases, hoping one would stick
And said she robbed places that didn't exist
In the midst of threats on her life and being caged with Aryan whites
Through dark halls of hate she carried the light
I wonder what would happen if that woulda been me?
All of this shit so we could be free.
Yeah, I often wonder what would happen if that woulda been me?
All of this shit so we could be free, so dig it, people-

(Cee-Lo)
I'm thinkin' of Assata, yeah.
Listen to my Love, Assata, yeah.
Your Power and Pride, so Beautiful...
May God bless your Soul.
Oooh.

(Common)
Yo
From North Carolina her grandmother would bring
news that she had had a dream

103

Her dreams always meant what they needed them to mean
What made them real was the action in between
She dreamt that Assata was free in they old house in Queens
The fact that they always came true was the thing
Assata had been convicted of a murder she couldna done
Medical evidence shown she couldna shot the gun
It's time for her to see the sun from the other side
Time for her daughter to be by her mother's side
Time for this Beautiful Woman to become soft again
Time for her to breathe, and not be told how or when
She untangled the chains and escaped the pain
How she broke out of prison I could never explain
And even to this day they try to get to her
but she's free with political asylum in Cuba.

(Cee-Lo vocals)
I'm thinkin' of Assata, yeah.
Listen to my Love, Assata, yeah.
We're molded from the same mud, Assata.
We share the same Blood, Assata, yeah.
Your Power and Pride, so Beautiful...
May God bless your Soul.
Your Power and Pride, so Beautiful...
May God bless your Soul.
Oooh.

(Assata)
Freedom! You askin me about freedom. Askin me about freedom?
I'll be honest with you. I know a whole more about what freedom isn't
than about what it is, cause I've never been free.
I can only share my vision with you of the future, about what freedom is.
Uhh, the way I see it, freedom is-- is the right to grow, is the right to
blossom.
Freedom is -is the right to be yourself, to be who you are,
to be who you wanna be, to do what you wanna do.

Lesson 2: International Geography

Exploring International Geography through Hip-Hop

Author(s): Daniel D. Zarazua

Bio: Daniel D. Zarazua is currently teaching social studies at Unity High School in Oakland, CA and his teaching experience includes Stanford's Upward Bound Program and the University of Michigan where he received his M.A. in Secondary Education. He's currently serving on the Education Committee of H²Ed, an organization devoted to integrating hip hop into the classroom. Additionally, he's a coordinator for the DJ Project, an arts and entrepreneurial youth program.

Grades: 9-12   **Subjects:** Social Studies, Global Studies

Academic Content Standards: Geography Standard 4- Understands the physical and human characteristics of place. Geography Standard 10- Understands the nature and complexity of Earth's cultural mosaics. Geography Standard 13- Understands the forces of cooperation and conflict that shape the divisions of Earth's surface. Music Standard 7- Understands the relationship between music and history and culture

Overview of Lesson Plan: An extended warm-up exercise to show the global influence of hip hop and as a way to engage students about historical and cultural facts. After identifying the location, they needed to identify and label them on a map. This activity can be used as a springboard for numerous discussions.

Suggested Time Allowance: One Hour

Objectives: Students will:
1. Become more familiar with the location of international cities and countries.
2. Increase their awareness of the history and/or culture of various countries.
3. Increase their awareness of how popular culture is shaped by many influences.

Resources / Materials:
-Copies of "International Hip Hop" geography questions
-Copies of blank world map (http://www.eduplace.com/ss/maps/pdf/world_country.pdf)
-reference materials (encyclopedias, maps, computers with Internet access, newspapers and magazines)

Background:
As with most teachers, I noticed that while many of my students did not know have basic skills in areas such as geography they had a good grasp of popular culture. This lesson was designed to tap into this knowledge while teaching them core academic skills. The students work in groups and really enjoyed this activity. The students who know a lot about hip hop can contribute if their

academic skills are weaker and the students who aren't big hip hop fans can contribute if they are stronger in academic areas. Fortunately, all of my students fall in either or both of these categories.

Activities / Procedures:

1. Warm up activity: Working individually, students will answer the following question on a sheet of paper: Make a list of anything that you use in your life that comes from another country or was made in another country. This can include music, fashion, language, cars, video games, etc. Students then share their responses.

2. As a class, discuss how our lives are connected to a global community in areas that we take for granted, including music.

3. Break students up into small groups and hand out geography questions. As they work on these questions they should be filling in the maps.

4. Go over correct answers as a class and discuss students' thoughts about the information.

5. Wrap up: Students will be given a quiz the following day to test their knowledge of various cities and countries and/or key facts about each. For extra credit students can color in maps and do additional research on select countries or information.

Further Questions for Discussion:

1. Is there any such things a "pure" culture?

2. What are some ways that other groups have borrowed or learned from the students' culture?

3. What are some ways that the students' friends or community have borrowed or learned from other cultures?

Evaluation / Assessment:
Participation in class, completion of map, and quiz.

Vocabulary:
Ancestor, colonialism, continent, Creole, culture, descent, diplomat, ethnic, export, import, national, revolt,

Extension Activities:
Have students design their own quizzes. They can research topics of their choice to help generate questions.

Students create and label their own maps with interesting facts or themes such as origins of their favorite music artists or genres, famous athletes, etc.

Hip Hop Geography (International)

By <u>Daniel D. Zarazua</u>

An exercise I used to show the global influence of hip hop and as a way to engage students about historical and cultural facts. The students worked in groups and really enjoyed this activity. The students who knew a lot about hip hop could contribute if their academic skills were weaker and the students who weren't big hip hop fans could contribute if they were stronger in the academic areas. Fortunately, all of my students fell in either or both of these categories. After identifying the location, they needed to identify it on a map. Numerous discussions arose from information that was listed in this activity. Please note that these questions should be updated from time to time to keep the info relevant as new artists come out everyday.

1. Panjabi MC, who recently did a track with Jay-Z, has ancestors who are from this sub-continent near Asia and the Middle East.

2. Orishas are divine beings worshiped by the Yoruba in West Africa. Because of the slave trade, they are also worshipped in the Americas in religions such as Santeria. The hip hop group Orishas is from an island that is known for Santeria, as well as Fidel Castro.

3. The Zulu Nation was formed by Afrika Bambaataa in the 1970's to promote hip hop and help combat gang violence. The Zulus were famous for resisting British colonialism in Africa in the 1800s. They currently live in this African country known for apartheid and Nelson Mandela.

4. Big Pun, Fat Joe, and J. Lo's cultural roots are from this Caribbean Island whose name means "rich port" in Spanish.

5. Kardinal Offishall is from the "T Dot," which is a city located in a country known for its "mounties." This city has a professional sports team called the Blue Jays. What is the city and country?

6. DJ Honda is from this small island country which is known for import cars and Godzilla. The United States also dropped atomic bombs on two of its major cities, ending World War II.

7. Jin of the Ruff Ryders, the Mountain Brothers, and Chris Wong Won (Fresh Kid Ice) of the 2 Live Crew share ancestors from the same country as Bruce Lee, Yao Ming, and Jackie Chan. What is this country?

8. The name of 50 Cent's neighborhood shares a name with a country known for its national music of reggae.

9. Wyclef Jean and Pras are from this French Creole speaking island that is also known for a major slave revolt in the 1800s.

10. The video for Snoop Dogg's "Beautiful" video was filmed in what country? Hint: This

107

country has the largest population of people of African descent in the world.

11. When Aaliyah passed away, she died in a plane crash after filming a video in this island country that rhymes with "Da Mamas."

12. Busta Rhymes, Funkmaster Flex, and the Notorious B.I.G. are just a few of the rappers who share the same motherland as Bob Marley; which is?

13. Many of the most well-known DJs are from the San Francisco Bay area. Incidentally, a high number of them have ancestors from this island country in the Pacific, whose culture is often called a cousin of Spanish and Latino culture. This country is also known for dishes such as pancit and lumpia.

14. Even when breakdancing stopped being a fad, crews such as The Rocksteady Crew kept it alive. Many members, including Crazy Legs are ethnically of the same background as people such as Ricky Martin, J. Lo and Benito Santiago of the San Francisco Giants. What island country are their families from?

15. DJ Nick Toth, MC Maya Jupiter, and Koolism are from the only country that is also a continent. What is it?

16. Mystikal and Shaggy fought for the United States in a Middle East conflict that is currently being repeated in which country?

17. Talib Kweli and Mos Def formed a group called Black Star, which comes from the name of a shipping line started by Marcus Garvey, an African-American leader of the 1920s. Besides places such as the United States and Jamaica, Garvey was active in this European country known for Winston Churchill, Princess Diana, and Monty Python.

18. M.C. Solar is from a key European country (not Germany) who disagreed with the United States' attack on Iraq. This country is also famous for escargot and one of its towers.

19. The Bay area's DJ Vlad is from this country, which was the U.S.'s enemy in the Cold War.

20. The Beastie Boys share a religious background whose homeland is surrounded by Arab countries. This country is the only non-Muslim country in the region and has had major conflicts with Palestine since it was formed.

21. Dancehall reggae superstar Buju Banton is known for doing hip hop mixes with mcs including Big Pun. He is also known for being very pro-African and often mentions this eight-lettered African country that starts with a "B".

22. Sydney, Australia-based DJ Nick Toth is the son of a diplomat of Arnold Schwarzenegger's home country. What is this country?

23. Both DMX and Aaliyah starred in a movie with Jet Li who is from which former British colony?

24. Wyclef Jean produced a song for Carlos Santana. Which border town (U.S. and Mexican border) is Santana from? Hint: many U.S. Marines get arrested in this city.

25. The group House of Pain scored a big hit with "Jump Around." Although they're an American-based group they strongly represented the culture of which country? Hint: The northern part of this country is actually governed by England and is known for its conflicts between Catholics and Protestants.

26. Shyne moved with his mother to New York from this small English-speaking country next to Mexico.

27. Charli Baltimore is bi-racial. Her father is African-American and her mother is from this European country known as the birthplace of the Nazi party and whose capital used to be divided by a wall.

28. Lumidee's parents are from this Caribbean country which shares an island with Haiti and is home to merengue music.

29. Carlos Santana and Mellow Man Ace remade and sampled, respectively, Latin percussionist Tito Puente's "Oye Como Va." Tito's home land is a U.S. territory and recently home to protests against practice bombings by the United States Navy.

30. Lil' John sports dreads and used to remix reggae songs. Both dreads and reggae are associated with the Rastafarian religion. Which East African country do Rastas revere due to it being the birthplace of their spiritual leader Hallie Selassie?

31. DJ Craze is from a Central American country that some people closely link to the rise in the drug trade in South Central Los Angeles. There is a theory that the CIA helped fund the drug trade in South Central to help raise money for rebels to overthrow the government of this country, that starts with the letter "N".

Hip Hop Geography KEY
International

1. India
2. Cuba
3. South Africa
4. Puerto Rico
5. Toronto, Canada
6. Japan
7. China
8. Jamaica
9. Haiti
10. Brazil
11. Bahamas
12. Jamaica
13. Philippines
14. Puerto Rico
15. Australia
16. Iraq
17. England
18. France
19. Russia
20. Israel
21. Botswana
22. Austria
23. Hong Kong
24. Tijuana
25. Ireland
26. Belize
27. Germany
28. Dominican Republic
29. Puerto Rico
30. Ethiopia
31. Nicaragua

Lesson 3: What Prophet?

Author(s): Andrew Landers

Bio: Andrew Landers owes unlimited gratitude to his brothers for, among other things, the influence of Hip-Hop on his life. Co-Leader of the Hip-Hop Association's Education Committee, A. holds a Masters Degree in Literacy from The City College of New York and graduated from Boston University's School of Education. Now with five years experience teaching students with special needs in NYC public schools, A. has been an educator since 1995.

Objective: Each student will build vocabulary and produce a creative written/visual piece based on the idea of being a superhero for his/her community.

Grades: 6-8, 9-12   **Subject Areas:** Language Arts

Academic Content Standards: Language Arts Standard 1- Demonstrates competence in the general skills and strategies of the writing process. Language Arts Standard 4- Gathers and uses information for research purposes. Language Arts Standard 7- Demonstrates competence in the general skills and strategies for reading a variety of informational texts. Music Standard 7- Understands the relationship between music and history and culture. Language Arts Standard 2- Demonstrates competence in the stylistic and rhetorical aspects of writing. Language Arts Standard 8- Demonstrates competence in speaking and listening as tools for learning.

Description: After listening to and discussing the song, "You Can't Stop the Prophet", by Jeru the Damaja, each student will identify his/herself as a particular hero to the community he/she lives in and what 'enemies' are providing a battle against progress and positivity.

Target Audience: This activity will be most useful to teachers, students, and youth who are conscious or seeking to be conscious about the struggles of their community.
Resources / Materials:
1. "You Can't Stop the Prophet", by Jeru the Damaja; The Sun Rises in the East, Payday Records, 1994
2. Copy of transcribed lyrics. (www.ohhla.com)
3. Worksheets 1 & 2 (attached)

Activities / Procedures: Discuss and define words (Worksheet 1). Specifically: What does it mean to be ignorant?
-Listen to "You Can't Stop the Prophet" and discuss the events and meaning of the song. Chart significant responses and facts such as: "prophet is the hero", "young kids are having babies", etc.
-Listen to "You Can't Stop the Prophet" with the lyrics.
-Complete and discuss Worksheet 2.
-Begin plans based on the project goal.
Evaluation: Student projects will clearly establish a hero or heroine fighting with a particular cause. Forces to be improved or changed are specifically identified and thoughtfully explained.

111

Can't Stop the Prophet

Ignorance hates when I drop it,

But no matter what he do, he...

Can't Stop the Prophet. (Project Goal)

In Jeru the Damaja's song, "You Can't Stop the Prophet," the Prophet is in a battle against Mr. Ignorance and his boys. Using his "knowledge of self" and "super scientifical" powers, the Prophet fights despair, animosity, deception, and other forces afflicting him and his people.

In a creative format that could be, but is not limited to poetry, song verse, short story, or cartoon, you will identify yourself as a hero/heroine, and explain what it is that you would fight against.

WHAT WOULD YOU, AS A PROPHET, FIGHT AGAINST AND WHY?
HOW?

Can't Stop the Prophet Worksheet 1

Define the following words:

1. ignorance:

2. prophet:

3. nemesis:

4. hate:

5. jealousy:

6. envy:

7. despair:

8. animosity:

9. deceit:

10. saga:

Can't Stop the Prophet Worksheet 2

1. Who are the two main characters in this battle?

2. Where, according to the song, is this battle taking place?

3. Name two weapons used by the prophet.

4. Name two behaviors that have earned Mr. Ignorance his name.

5. This story is a fantasy, but there are many realities that compare to the world we live in. Name two.

6. In two sentences, give your opinion of the song titled "YouCan't Stop the Prophet" by Jeru the Damaja.

7. The story ends with the Prophet in "a bit of a jam." In no less than five sentences, write a conclusion to this story.

Artist: Jeru the Damaja

Album: The Sun Rises in the East

Song: You Can't Stop the Prophet

Typed by: OHHLA Webmaster DJ Flash

Guy 1: Ohhh! Yo look towards the darkness

Guy 2: Nah nah yo, look towards the light

Guy 1: Yo what! Oh what the? Yo what is that?

Guy 2: It's a supernova

Guy 1: Nah nah man, that's a black hole

Guy 2: Yo! Yo!

Guy 1: Yo!

1 + 2: Yo it's... IT'S... IT'S?!!!

[The Prophet]

I, leap over lies in a single bound (Who are you?)

The Black Prophet

One day I got struck by Knowledge of Self

It gave me super-scientifical powers

Now I, run through the ghetto

Battlin my, arch nemesis Mr. Ignorance

He's been tryin' to take me out since the days of my youth

He feared this day would come

116

I'm hot on his trail, but sometimes he slips away

Because he has an army, they always give me trouble

Mainly - Hatred, Jealousy and Envy they attack me

They think they got me

But I use my super-science and I twist all three

I see sparks over that buildin' - they're shootin' at me

I dip, do a backflip

Then hit em in the heart with sharp steel bookmarks

Ignorance hates when I drop it

But no matter, what he do... he can't stop the Prophet

[Deceit]

Yo Prophet, yo Prophet, c'mere real quick

Yo I just saw Ignorance downtown, let me put you on

[Girl #2]

Word, he down there buggin'

He got them ill in out, they shootin'' and everything else...

[The Prophet]

Let's continue the saga, mad mad drama

I met this chick, she said she knew where Ignorance was at

I said, "Where?"

She said, "Downtown"

He had babies havin' babies - and young niggaz sellin' crack

I think the b**** is lyin', it's a set up

I can smell it, but Ignorance is runnin' rampant

Aight baby show me the exact spot

Meet me at Hoyt and Schermerhorn at 3 on the dot

So I hops up on the A-Train, I'm bein' followed

My seventh sense senses danger

I turn around, it's Anger

and he brought a mob along, it's the same old song

Despair and Animosity got broke with the swiftness

I don't know what they think this is

I feel a sharp pain in my neck

Now I can't see, I'm like Hiram

They hit me with the dart filled with the pork chop serum

I tried to hold on but before long I dropped

When I awoke I was locked in the barber's shop

Trapped in the barber's chair

Oh no, they're gonna try and cut my hair

But that can't stop the Prophet

[Anger]

Yo Prophet!

Ignorance is tired of you followin' him around

We about to put an end to that RIGHT NOW

Animosity (YEA!) Despair (YO WHASSUP?) Get him!!

{DJ Premier cuts and scratches: "Can't a damn thing stop me"}

[The Prophet]

A few minutes passed by, I hear a buzzin' noise

It was that chick with some of Ignorance's boys

She said, "Prophet, we got you beat;

by the way I'm Mr. Ignorance's wife, Deceit.

But enough talk; now for your hair cut.."

When the clippers touched my hair, they blew the F*** up

After the explosion there was no one left

Cause I know Dim Mak/poison hand/touch of death

My vision's still kinda blurry, but I see a clue

Ignorance is at the library

I hurry, with lightning speed like The Flash

He's at the big one, on Grand, Army Plaz'

When I get inside the doors shut and the lights go off

Damn, another trap

I hear a hissin sound, I smell a funny smell

I gasp, I can't breathe

Ignorance is laughin' at me

Waitin' on my downfall, but he can't stop the Prophet

[Mr. Ignorance]

Well Prophet

It seems like you're in a bit of a jam

I hope you can unstick yourself

Oh, and what you did to my wife, it was nothing

I have others

Hahahahahaha... hahahahaha.. hahahahahah...

"The saga continues!"

Lesson 4: *Who Am I?* Using DNA to Determine Ancestry and Cultural Identity

Author (s): Gina Paige, African Ancestry (www.africanancestry.com for more information)

AFRICAN ANCESTRY
trace your dna. find your roots.

Overview of the lesson: In this lesson students will learn about the process of tracing African ancestry through DNA, as well as through historical and cultural artifacts. Students will learn about the global significance of African ancestry on the Hip-Hop music and culture.

Grades: 9-12   **Subjects**: World History, Science, Language Arts, Geography

Science Standard 5- Understands the genetic basis for the transfer of biological characteristics from one generation to the next. Science Standard 6- Knows the general structure and functions of cells in organisms. Science Standard 14- Understands the nature of scientific knowledge. Science Standard 16- Understands the scientific enterprise. Language Arts Standard 1- Demonstrates competence in the general skills and strategies of the writing process. Language Arts Standard 4- Gathers and uses information for research purposes. Geography Standard 10 - Understands the nature and complexity of Earth's cultural mosaics. Geography Standard 13 - Understands the forces of cooperation and conflict that shape the divisions of Earth's surface. World History Standard 43- Understands how post-World War II reconstruction occurred, new international power relations took shape, and colonial empires broke up. World History Standard 44 - Understands the search for community, stability, and peace in an interdependent world.

Objectives:

Students will:

1. Understand the science of how their DNA can be used to determine their mother's and father's genetic heritage.

2. Understand why African Americans must use genetic ancestry tracing as a supplement to genealogical research

122

H²Ed

3.Understand how knowing one's ancestry can be impactful on a personal, national, and global level.

 4. Create a family tree.

Activities/Procedures:

1.Warm-Up/Do-Now: As students enter class, hand out the following questionnaire (photocopied before class):

Who are you? How would you describe yourself? How do you view yourself? Where are you from?

I am _____ (Have students name as many things as they can think of…)

I am from _____

After students have completed their list, quickly determine which types of descriptors or categories come up the most often and present them to the class for discussion. Did anyone refer to him/herself as African? Why or why not? Does anyone view himself or herself as having African Ancestry and not write that down? The discussion is about how we identify ourselves; and the impact that being of African descent has on sense of self.

2. Show an ancestry-related video:

African Ancestry DVD presentation of how DNA is used to trace ancestry to the class (Science oriented) (available at africanancestry.com)

DVD of the Judge Hatchett Show where a young man traces his ancestry using DNA (Sociology oriented) (may have to order from the television show)

Chris Tucker or Oprah Winfrey segment of PBS' African American Lives (History oriented) (available on pbs.org)

3. Discuss what characteristics we have from our families that are genetic (nature) vs. learned (nurture). There is a list of notable African Americans who have traced their ancestries. Using all available resources students can research these people and identify relationships between their lives and their African ancestries.

   Louis Gossett Jr. (Sierra Leone)

   Jim Brown (Nigeria)

   Hill Harper (Nigeria)

   Kimberly Elise (Mali)

   Vanessa Williams *from the TV series Soul Food* (Cameroon)

Isaiah Washington (Sierra Leone)

Forrest Whitaker (Ghana)

Chris Tucker (Angola)

Oprah Winfrey (Liberia)

Quincy Jones (Cameroon)

Robin Roberts *Good Morning America* (Liberia)

Former Ambassador Andrew Young (Sierra Leone)

Dr. Dorothy Height (Sierra Leone)

Congresswoman Diane Watson D-CA (Central African Republic)

Congresswoman Barbara Lee D-CA (Guinea and Sierra Leone)

Bishop T.D. Jakes (Nigeria)

Dr. Ben Carson (Kenya and Mozambique)

4. Discuss the reasons why African Americans cannot point to a country of origin and show how despite the disconnection, cultural elements have been passed down throughout generations. Have students watch a film about the MAAFA or Transatlantic Slave Trade such as *Amistad* or *Roots*, and write an essay on how internalized oppression and legacies of slavery are still prominent in Hip-Hop culture today.

5. Have students identify elements of our culture stem from our African ancestry; particularly as they relate to Hip-Hop culture (music, drums, language sayings, hairstyles, dance, names, foods) and research the African countries in which they are found.

Interdisciplinary Connections: Determine which other countries in the world have large numbers of people of African descent. Study the African cultural elements in those countries.

-Have students calculate the number of ancestors they have at each generation. Using statistics in the presentation about African Ancestry's results, have students calculate the percentage of results by African country or by US state.

6. **Wrap-Up/Homework**: Have students create their family trees and identify all of the people that they share maternal ancestry with and those that they share paternal ancestry with. Determine who in their family would have to provide DNA in order to determine ancestry.

Vocabulary: DNA, mitochondrial DNA, Y chromosome, genetics, ancestry, lineage, identity, inherit, descendant, sequence

II. MUSIC, MATHEMATICS AND SCIENCE

Music has been used since the beginning of time to teach mathematics as well as other academic disciplines, these lessons combine the knowledge of beats, rhymes, and dance with the complexity of advanced level math and science.

- **Lesson 1: The Number Line Dance**

    Author(s): Alex Kajitani

Do The Math...

- **Lesson 2: Applied Travel Math: Applying Math Skills in an International Context**

    Author(s): Daniel Zarazua

- **Lesson 3: Microphone Check 1,2 1,2 Using Hip Hop to Review Math Skills**

    Author(s): Andrew J. Ryan

- **Lesson 4: Break Dancing and the Muscular System**

    Author(s): Tatiana Forero Puerta

- **Song: "The Science Chant"**

    Author(s): Ron Kelly, Edutainment

Song: "I Can Read More Than You"

    Author(s): Ron Kelley, Edutainment

The Numbers:

In 2005....

26%	The percentage of Black people age 16 and older who work in management, professional and related occupations.
44,000	The number of Black physicians and surgeons
79,400	The number of Black postsecondary teachers
45,200	The number of Black lawyers
49,300	The number of Black chief executives.

2005 American Community Survey and Upcoming Statistical Abstract of the United States: 2007, Table 602.

Lesson 1: The Number Line Dance!

Author(s): Alex Kajitani

Bio: Alex Kajitani, aka *The Rappin' Mathematician*™ is a middle school math teacher in San Diego, California. Though his students come from one of the poorest neighborhoods in San Diego, they consistently outperform district averages on benchmark exams. The students often cite his "Math Raps" as the reason for their high level of motivation and performance. He recently released "Volume 1," a collection of songs to help students enjoy math, rap music, and positive messages. He enjoys spending time with his wife and daughter, and is an avid surfer. For more information, visit www.MathRaps.com

Grades: 5-8   **Subject**: Mathematics

Academic Content Standards: Music Standard 7- Understands the relationship between music and history and culture. Mathematics Standard 1- Uses a variety of strategies in the problem-solving process. Mathematics Standard 7- Understands and applies basic and advanced concepts of probability. Mathematics Standard 9- Understands the general nature and uses of mathematics

Overview of Lesson: The Number Line Dance is an effective, fun way to help students conceptualize and apply positive and negative integers. Negative numbers are often difficult for students in basic math classes, because it is their first glimpse into more "theoretical" numbers. This lesson is also a great way to get students moving, singing, and dancing around!

Suggested Time: One hour

Objective: The students will be able to understand positive and negative numbers, and apply them to real-world situations involving profit and debt.

Resources: Pencils; paper; ruler; masking tape; an open, flat surface, a copy of *The Rappin' Mathematician's* song, **The Number Line Dance** (optional), available at www.MathRaps.com.

Activities/Procedures:

1. Warm Up: Begin by having students complete a quick-write (about one paragraph) about a time that they needed to borrow some money, or, a time in which they lent some money to a friend. How much money did they need/lend? What was it for? How long did it take to pay back/get paid back?

2. Explain to students that they will be doing "The Number Line Dance." In order to do so, they will first need to create their number line. Using masking tape, have them place a long strip of tape on the ground, in a straight line. Lengths of line will vary. Have them use a ruler to evenly space out the numbers. *Suggestion:* have them do the origin (zero) first, then the numbers going in the positive and negative directions. Going to -10 to the left of the origin, and +10 to the right, should be sufficient. Advanced learners may

choose to go higher in both directions.

3. After the number lines have been constructed, have the students stand at the origin (zero). Explain that they will be doing **The Number Line Dance:** *Negative to the left, positive to the right, it's the number line, dance, and I could dance all night!!!* Explain that the teacher will be reading a situation about a student who spends and earns money. Every time the student spends money, that is considered a negative expense, and the students should move to the left. Each time the students earn money, that is considered a positive, and they should move to the right. It is best to practice a few times with positive/negative numbers, before launching into numbers that deal with money. For example, the teacher can call out -3: and the students move 3 spaces to the left; followed by +7, in which the students will move 7 spaces to the right. The teacher can then ask the students where they are- most will anxiously call out +4!

4. Several times throughout the activity, the teacher should shout out one line of the chorus, and the students should shout out the following line. For example:

   Teacher: *Negative to the left!*

   Students: *Positive to the right!*

   Teacher: *It's the number line dance,*

   Students: *And I could dance all night!*

5. The following situation should be read by the teacher: Feel free to modify it as you see fit:

   > *Jose is hanging out with his friends. They decide to go to the taco shop to eat lunch. Unfortunately, Jose does not have any money; however, he does have a very nice friend, who offers to loan him $5. Jose accepts, and eats up all of his tacos (students move 5 spaces to the left). On the way home, Jose and his friends decide that they are still hungry, and stop for ice cream. Jose borrows another $3, and orders 2 scoops of "cookies and cream" ice cream. Yummy! (students move 3 more spaces to the left). When he gets home, he has no money to pay his friend back, so his mom suggests he get a job. His neighbor, Bob, offers to give Jose a job washing cars, for $2 per car. Jose accepts the job, and washes 4 cars that afternoon (students move 8 spaces to the right). How much money does Jose now have? He may have $8 from washing cars, but he still has to pay his friend back! The next day, his friends come over to pick Jose up. They are going to the mall. However, Jose decides not to go with them, and goes to his new job instead, where he washes 5 cars. (Students move 10 spaces to the right) How much money does Jose now have? What should he do with his $10?*

The above scenario can be modified, extended, or shortened to meet the needs of your students. After each time the students move, I like to call out "Negative to the left…" and have the students answer the next line together. They absolutely love "The Number Line Dance!" The complete, hip-hop version of this song is available at www.MathRaps.com.

Follow up activity: Have students write their own scenarios about earning, spending, going into debt, and play them out with a partner. Similar scenarios can also be used regarding positive and negative temperatures; football teams gaining and losing yardage in a football game; and traveling above/below sea level.

Lesson 2: Applied Travel Math

Applying math skills in an international context

Author(s): Daniel D. Zarazua

Bio: Daniel D. Zarazua is currently teaching social studies at Unity High School in Oakland , CA and his teaching experience includes Stanford's Upward Bound Program and the University of Michigan where he received his M.A. in Secondary Education. He's currently serving on the Education Committee of H^2Ed, an organization devoted to integrating hip hop into the classroom. Additionally, he's a coordinator for the DJ Project, an arts and entrepreneurial youth program.

Grades: 6-8   **Subjects:** Mathematics

Academic Content Standards: Music Standard 7- Understands the relationship between music and history and culture. Mathematics Standard 1- Uses a variety of strategies in the problem-solving process. Mathematics Standard 7- Understands and applies basic and advanced concepts of probability. Mathematics Standard 9- Understands the general nature and uses of mathematics

Overview of Lesson Plan: Students will apply basic math skills and critical thinking skills based on a sample trip to Europe.

Suggested Time Allowance: One Hour

Objectives:
Students will:
1. Apply key math skills, including multiplication, conversions, negative numbers and multi-step problems.
2. Increase awareness of key historical events and geographical locations.

3. Contemplate real-life-money-management issues.

Resources / Materials:
-Copies of hand out (attached)

Background:
Like most teachers I try to make material as relevant to students' lives as possible. When it comes to applied math I often try to use problems and references that they can relate to, such as products that they buy or are interested in. Additionally, I try to work in more subtle lessons or be cross-disciplinary. In this case particular case I referenced topics that we studied in other subjects and I wanted them to see themselves as world travelers.

Activities / Procedures:
1. Warm up activity: Start off asking students some basic questions, such as what is the farthest

they have ever traveled. I briefly ask them questions about their experience, before segueing into more math-oriented questions; how much do they think it cost to fly to Europe, how far away is England from here, how would they entertain themselves, etc.

2. Then hand out the worksheet and allow them to work.

3. Once it appears that nearly everyone is finished, go over the problems and discuss their thoughts on the questions.

4. Wrap up: Tell students to imagine where they would like to travel and to develop a backdrop or characters for this trip. For example, this class work included a DJ. As a group, brainstorm questions that they can create. For their homework students will begin to create their own applied-math problems around topics that you have suggested, as well as ones they come up with themselves. Some examples include temperature, calories taken in, and money conversion. They should research key facts for homework and finalize their applied lesson plans in class.

Further Questions for Discussion:
1. If a person does not know how to do math, what kinds of problems will they encounter if they travel?

Evaluation / Assessment:
Participation in class, completion worksheet, creation of own applied-math problems.

Vocabulary:
Distance, round trip

Extension Activities:
1. Have students continue to design their own applied math problems.

2. Have students document trips on blank maps to help with their geography skills. For example, they can trace where the trip takes them, create a legend describing climate changes, the costs of goods, etc.

1. The flight from San Francisco to Amsterdam takes 10 hours. To entertain passengers the airline shows various movies and television shows. Based on the information given, approximately how much total time was used and how much time was left over? (4 pts)

Out of Time movie (88 minutes)

Pietje Bell movie (110 minutes)

News (40 minutes)

Everybody Loves Raymond (20 minutes)

Discovery Channel program (25 minutes)

2. The distance from San Francisco to Amsterdam is 5466 miles each way. If you take 7 round trips, how many miles would you travel all together? (2 pts)

3. As the airplane gains altitude it gets colder outside with temperature dropping to as low as –62 degrees. If the current temperature in Oakland is +58 degrees, what's the difference in temperature? (2 pts)

4. The in-flight magazine featured an article on children with AIDS in Romania who are abandoned by their families. There are about 8,700 of these children who are placed into group homes. Each home holds 18 kids and costs 29,000 European dollars to operate each year. Approximately how many homes will be needed? How much money will be needed to complete these homes? (4 pts)

5. Many of the pay telephones at European airports also have internet access which costs 3 European dollars to use for every 15 minutes. How much would it cost to use the internet for one hour?
(2 pts)

6. The flight from Amsterdam to London takes 50 minutes. If you took a return trip, how much total time would you spend in the air? (2 pts)

7. A train connects London, England and Paris, France, running underneath the ocean. The cost for a round-trip ticket is $90. How much would it cost to take this trip 3 times? (2 pts)

8. The church of Notre Dame in Paris (home of the fabled Hunchback of Notre Dame) sells candles as one way to make money for upkeep. If you spent 18 European dollars on candles that cost 3 European dollars each, how many candles did you buy? (2 pts)

9. A few hundred years ago, the cemeteries in Paris became overcrowded and the bodies had to be removed. As a result, a series of tunnels, known as the catacombs, were built 65 feet underneath the city for storage. There are 6 million skeletons stored down there. If

there were a plan to relocate these skeletons over the course of 15 years, how many would need to be removed per year if an equal amount is removed each year? (2 pts)

10. A group of friends go out to eat in Paris and buy the following items. How much money do they spend altogether? (2 pts)

2 steak dinners at $12 each

1 Gumbo at $10

1 Duck stew at $10

4 Drinks at $3 each

1 order of snail appetizers at $8

2 ice creams at $4 each

1 Sorbet at $4

11. A French DJ goes to the music store to update her collection. If she buys the following items, what is her final bill? (2 pts)

Beyonce' record, $9 Laurant Guanier record, $6

Yung Joc record, $9 Lucian single, $6

Outkast record, $9 DJ Koyote mix CD, $10

Bob Marley album, $15

12. A club promoter is calculating how much money he made on the night. Given the following figures, how much did he make? 115 women at $7 each and 135 men at $10 each (2 pts)

13. Unemployed French men over the age of 25 receive 600 European dollars per month. How much do they receive per year? (2 pts)

14. While in Paris, a young man decides to buy a new outfit. He sees the following items in the store: Iverson tennis shoes ($150), Ecko pullover ($120), Dickie jeans ($140), and a Tommy Hilfiger watch ($200). How much would he end up spending altogether? (2 pts)

15. This same guy sees roundtrip tickets from San Jose to Paris for $450. Would he be able to afford a return trip to Paris if he chooses to not buy this 'fit? (2 pts)

16. If this same fellow's rent back home in Union City is $800 per month, what is the difference between the amount he might spend on these clothes and the cost to keep a roof over his head?
(2 pts)

Lesson 3: Microphone Check: 1,2 1, 2 . . .

Using Hip-Hop to Review Math Skills

Author(s): Andrew J. Ryan

Bio: Andrew J. Ryan is the Executive Director of Hip-Hop Matters, and the founding editor in chief of the Journal of Hip-Hop. Raised in the Bronx New York, the former systems engineer left a promising research career to focus on his true passion. Ryan teaches courses on Hip-Hop at both George Mason University and the University of the District of Columbia.

CollegeBound Teen Magazine named Ryan's first Hip-Hop course: "Beats, Rhyme and Culture", at #14 in their list of the top 25 'coolest' college courses. In addition to his work at the university level, Ryan has taught math at both the high school and middle school level in Washington DC. He is the author of "The Responsible Use of Hip-Hop in the Classroom" published by Peter Lang due out in the fall of 2007.

Grades: 6-8, 9-12

Subjects: Math, History

Academic Content Standards: Music Standard 7- Understands the relationship between music and history and culture. Mathematics Standard 1- Uses a variety of strategies in the problem-solving process. Mathematics Standard 7- Understands and applies basic and advanced concepts of probability. Mathematics Standard 9- Understands the general nature and uses of mathematics

Overview of Lesson Plan: Over the years, Hip-Hop, known best for its musical element of rap music, has become a medium which is more often 'seen than heard.' Listeners who were once master's of decoding the textual messages in rap music, have downgraded to only analyzing the visual messages. In this lesson, students will analyze the message of rap music and Hip-Hop culture in parallel with direct instruction with math and reading skills.

Suggested Time Allowance: 90 minutes

Objectives:

Students will:

1 Learn about the mathematical concepts which accompany rap recording contracts such as percent, units and finding percents of numbers by multiplying decimals.

2. Students will write constructive response utilizing math vocabulary and terms.

3. Use higher order skills to analyze rap lyrics from Mos Def.

4. Students will read article "The Numbers Beyond the Bling" by Ward Harkavy

 and discuss statistics mentioned in the article.

135

Resources / Materials:

-pens/pencils

-paper

-classroom board

-copies of the article "The Numbers Beyond the Bling"

by Ward Harkavy, *Village Voice* -- January 25, 2005

http://www.villagevoice.com/news/0501,harkavy,59767,2.html (one per student)

-index cards

-Copy of lyrics of "Mathematics" by Mos Def, *Black on Both Sides* (1999). Copy of clean version of song, available from iTunes Music Stores .

Activities / Procedures:

1. WARM-UP/DO-NOW: For 6-8 → Provide math questions on percentages, fractions, ratios, or multiplying decimals. For instance: 1,000x0.25 | ¾ of 500 | 75% of 400 | Choose problems which can be revisited within the lesson.

For 9-12 → Provide the following scenario on an overhead or handout.

You are the manager for a new Hip-Hop/R&B group which has just been offered the opportunity to submit 2 songs for the soundtrack of a Hollywood movie. You are offered a guarantee of $15,000 for each song or a 5% royalty on each CD sold. Your research shows CD sales have been declining and last year's best selling soundtrack sold 400,000 units. Your goal is to make as much money as possible for the group as you receive 10% of their earnings.

Describe mathematically how you would figure out the best choice for your group.

[after going over exercise, ask students to put themselves in the position of the recording studio. What is their reasoning in offering those terms?]

2. Direct instruction in math would prepare students for the exercise. Operations involving percentages, ratios, or fractions fit the best.

Alternatively, a history, economics, or law class may focus on issues involving royalties, publishing, and exploitive contracts. Website rapcoalition.org provides an excellent overview of rap's battle with record labels.

3. Lyrical Analysis -- Mos Def "Mathematics" – Mos Def differs from many rapper's due to the degree of social commentary in his music. Some students may know of Mos Def from his controversial concert at the MTV Video Music Awards, where he performed "Katrina Klap", a song about the injustices which occurred to the citizens of New Orleans after hurricane Katrina.

Mos Def has also starred on Broadway in Topdog/Underdog as well as several Hollywood movies. His versatility as a performer provides an opportunity to describe the intellect and talent which some rappers have. Others who fit this category include Nas, Common, Lauryn Hill, and Lupe Fiasco.

Print out lyrics from the song and use line numbering to denote each verse. For classes who have difficulty working independently, choose one stanza (16 lines) as opposed to the whole song. This will allow all students to relate to class discussion.

Have students work in groups of three to analyze lyrics. Ask students to circle any math terms or references to math. Once done, students should choose any 3 references and write a short summary describing the math behind the reference.

Ask for volunteers to share the math term they chose. There may be parts of the song which the students question or do not agree on. Remind them that the focus of the lesson is math, not lyrical accuracy. Also explain that lyrics, much like any writing, may have multiple meanings.

Use each math reference as an opportunity to review vocabulary or provide an rehabiliate a math skill. For instance,, Mos Def talks about the amount of profits which he keeps being 15%. Ask students to calculate his profits if his music grosses $20,000.

4. Read around. As a class, read and discuss the article "The Numbers Beyond the Bling"), http://www.villagevoice.com/news/0501,harkavy,59767,2.html

The article focuses on changes to American society since the early 1970's (roughly the time Hip-Hop first began). In a math context, discuss the concept of inflation and why prices were so different in the 1970s. In a historical reference, utilize venn diagrams to have students plot

10 items which were present in the 1970s versus today. Embed some of these items in previous lessons. You may provide a list of words to help the students get started.

For students in 6-8:

Focus on the mathematical concepts which are mentioned in the article. Use calculators to find answers to 'what if' scenarios. For example, if one statistic says unemployment was 12% in 1970 and is 6% in 2004, calculate the total difference based on US population.

5. WRAP-UP/HOMEWORK

Grade 6-8: Ask students to choose one statistic from the article or one math reference from the song and describe it mathematically. Students should use at least two math vocabulary words and provide an example using numbers.

Also assign students 5-7 math problems which relate to the concepts discussed in the lesson.

Grades 9-12: In an extended constructive, response (ECR), 5 to 7 sentences, describe how you would explain your decision to the group, who are not math experts like you.

Evaluation / Assessment:

Grades 6-8: Have students write the three most important points of the lesson on one side of an index card. On the other side, ask them to create their own math problem involving percent or decimals. Have students trade cards and attempt to answer their partner's question. Repeat if interest in the exercise is high.

On index cards, ask students to take either 1 math reference (no more than 3 lines) from Mos Def's "Mathematics" or one statistic from the article and describe its importance/meaning. Direct students to choose a reference which they can provide evidence to backup its authority.

Vocabulary:

Royalty, inflation, percent, tracking, Soundscan, recoup, profit, unit,

Extension Activities:

1. Have students research Nielsen Soundscan and the RIAA and the way each organization count record sales. Research can be done via the Internet and should be presented in a short essay.

2. Conduct an in-class debate on the influence of rap music on society. Some argue that rap music impacts people's behavior (especially youth), while other's say rap music is reporting on the conditions in which people live. Use the statistics from the article as a means to grounds the

student's comments.

3. Provide students with a list of values. Using an inflation calculator (The department of Labor homepage contains an excellent inflation calculator: http://www.bls.gov/bls/inflation.htm), have them find the equivalent dollar amount in various years. Ask students to hypothesize on why the values go up or down based on years.

4. Discuss the impact of downloading on artist royalties. Ask students to brainstorm on the reasons why downloading is important from the perspective of record companies, the artists, and the music consumer.

Other Information on the Web

Recording Industry of America (RIAA) – This trade group represents the US recording industry. [www.riaa.com]

Nielsen Soundscan – Nielsen Soundscan is the information system used by Billboard to determine record sales.

(http://www.soundscan.html).

Lesson 4: Break Dancing and the Muscular System

Investigating the human body through dance.

Author (s): Tatiana Forero Puerta

Bio: Tatiana Forero Puerta is part of the Education Team at the Tanenbaum Center for Interreligious Understanding in New York, where she develops tolerance-based curriculum. Tatiana has been involved in education for several years, teaching and volunteering in NY and CA, focusing on at-risk communities in East Palo Alto and West San Jose. Tatiana holds a dual B.A. in Philosophy and Religious studies from Stanford University and is currently finishing her M.A. at New York University in Continental Philosophy and Poetry.

Grades: 6-8   **Subjects:** Science, Health, Physical Education

Academic Content Standards: Physical Education Standard 5 - Understands the social and personal responsibility associated with participation in physical activity. Science Standard 14- Understands the nature of scientific knowledge. Science Standard 16- Understands the scientific enterprise. Health Standard 7- Knows how to maintain and promote personal health. Science Standard 6 - Knows the general structure and functions of cells in organisms. Health Standard 8 - Knows essential concepts about the prevention and control of disease.

Overview of Lesson Plan: Through video, pictures, discussion and activity, students will investigate the muscles in the human body through the study of the art of break dancing.

Suggested Time Allowance: 1.5 Hours

Objectives:
Students will:
1. Be able to list different positions in break dancing, as well historical information about the dance.
2. Be able to identify muscles in the body that are used in different break dancing poses
3. Research the use of muscles in different forms of dance

Resources/Materials:
-Break Dancing video (found at:
http://video.google.com/videoplay?docid=1766319080053392057&q=breakdance&hl=en)
-Break Dancing Information Handout (Included)
-Break Dancing Moves Handout (Included)
-Computer with projection
-Pens/pencils, Markers

-Notebook paper
-Classroom board
-Chalk or dry-erase markers
-Poster board or large paper

Activities/Procedures:
1. Warm-Up/Do-Now
Write down the following question on the board:
       "What is Break Dancing?"
Have students silently write down things they know about this dance form; this can be anything from what it looks like to where it comes from, etc (it can be in list format). Discuss answers with students.

2. After the discussion, distribute "Break Dance Information" handout provided. Read as a class (can have each student read one paragraph, going around the class). Ask students what they learned about break dancing from the handout.

3. Distribute "Break Dancing Moves" Handout, and ask students to read the descriptions of the moves quietly to themselves. Explain that they will watch a short video on break dancing, and that they should try to see if they recognize any of the moves that are on the handout.

4. Show the video.

5. Discuss what moves they recognized from the handout, or if they recognize any others that they may familiar with. Spark a discussion about what appears to be the most difficult aspect of the art form. See if the students recognize the physical agility and strength required.

6. Split students into four to six groups, depending on class size. Each group will be numbered 1 through 6. As a group, ask the students to look at their "Break Dancing Moves" handout. Each move pictured has a number next to it, at the bottom, right-hand corner of the picture of the move. The move with the number that is their group number belongs to that group respectively. Distribute "The Muscular System" handout. Each group will examine their corresponding move on "Break Dancing Moves" handout, while comparing it to "The Muscular System" handout.

7. In their groups, students are to analyze and discuss the particular muscles that are being used in their assigned move, by using "The Muscular System" handout as a guide. Distribute one piece of Poser Board/Paper per group. Students will draw a large sketch of their assigned move on the large poster paper, and will label the main muscles being used.

8. Students will present their moves with labeled muscles to the class, explaining why each muscle is on the chart (i.e. how do you know that muscle is being worked).

9. Students will go back to their desks and write down five muscles they did not know before.

4. Wrap-Up/Homework
1. Have students write about what other forms of dance, sports or physical activities they are

involved with. What muscles do you feel are worked? Is anything on your body sore after doing that exercise?

5. Further Questions for Discussion

1. How is Break Dancing similar to other forms of dance?
2. How is Break Dancing unique?
3. What forms of dance, sport or activity do you take part in? How does it impact different parts of your body?
4. What do you think it would take to become a good break dancer? Is this different than becoming a good dancer of another form of dance?

6. Evaluation/Assessment:

Students will be evaluated based on participation in discussions, the quality of their presentations (i.e. posters and the muscles labeled)

7. Vocabulary

Hip Hop, Toprock, Downrock, Freezing, Battles, Crews, B-boys, B-girls, 6-step, Moonwalk, Worm, Windmill, Headspin, Flare, Jackhammer.
Muscle names, i.e.: Trapezius, Deltoid, Triceps, Bicep, Latissimus Dorsi, Vastus Lateralis, Pectorals major, External Oblique, Rectus Abdominis, Sartorius, Quadricept.

8. Extension Activities

1. Students can research other forms of dance and the major muscles the art form impacts.
2. Have students look at the list of muscles they had not heard of before. Have each student choose two or three muscles, and research how that muscle works and what other types of activities engage that muscle.

Break Dancing

Break Dance, also known as breaking or b-boying, is a street dance style that evolved as part of the hip hop movement that originated among African American youths in the South Bronx of New York City during the early 1970s. It is arguably the best known of all hip hop dance styles.

Breaking is one of the four elements of hip-hop, the others being MCing, DJing, and graffiti.

Origins

Popular speculations of the early 1980s suggest that Break Dancing, in its organized fashion seen today, began as a method for rival gangs of the ghetto to mediate and settle territorial disputes. In a turn-based showcase of dance routines, the winning side was determined by the dancer(s) who could outperform the other by displaying a set of more complicated and innovative moves.

It later was through the highly-energetic performances of funk legend James Brown and the rapid growth of dance teams, like the Rock Steady Crew of New York City, that the competitive ritual of gang warfare evolved into a pop-culture phenomenon, receiving massive media attention. Parties, disco clubs, talent shows, and other public events became typical locations for Break Dancers, especially for gang members, where dancing served as a positive diversion from the threats of city life.

Though its intense popularity eventually faded in the 1980s, introduced street Break Dancing remains a mainstream phenomenon, maintaining exposure by the media through often comical portrayals in commercials and movies. For enthusiasts, breakdancing remains an enjoyable pastime and, for a few, a serious competitive dance where annual exhibitions and competitions of all levels take place.

Terminology

Toprock refers to any string of steps performed from a standing position, relying upon a mixture of coordination, flexibility, style, and most importantly, rhythm. Almost unorthodox-looking in general it is arguably the first and foremost opening display of style, a typical warm-up for transitions into more acrobatic maneuvers. Uprock is a competitively oriented type of toprock consisting of foot shuffles, spins, turns, and creative movements. Downrock, includes all footwork, such as 6 step or coffee grinder. More generally, a dancer's footwork refers his or her proficiency with foot speed and control.

Freezing, as the stationary name implicates, focuses on poses, the most skillful of which requires suspension off the floor using specific parts of the body. Whereas the said term refers to one pose, locking entails the sharp transition between each of multiple freezes, like clicks

143

associated with door bolts. Self-destructive moves are referred to as suicides and sees dancers landing safely (usually) in seemingly painful positions. Power moves include a wide range of moves that will obviously take a lot of power or strength. Some include Flare and Windmill.

Battles refer to any level of competition in which breakdancers, in an open space (typically a circle or square) participate in quick-paced, turn-based routines, whether improvised or planned. Participants vary in numbers, ranging from head-to-head duels to battles of opposing breakdance crews, or teams. Winners are determined by the side that exhibits the most proficient combinations of moves. Cyphers, on the other hand, are open-forum, mock exhibitions where competition is less emphasized.

The conventional breaking routine sees breakers transitioning from toprocking, to downrocking, typically with some variation of the foundational 6-step, and to a climactic freeze or suicide.

Break Dancing: The Basis

Top Rock Is a simple dance done standing up to initiate breakdancing. Its style is obvious to anyone watching, because it is incredibly unorthodox looking. Breakdancers take pride in having unique toprock that still stays within the definition of what toprock actually is.	
Uprock Is doing a toprock with someone else, sort of like a fight but without contact and very rhythmic. Uprocking is often confused with toprock, but the two are completely different dances.	
6-step 	Resembles walking in a circle on the ground. Only one hand is touching the ground at a time. The 6-step is the building block for the rest of the dance, and is heavily 'teched' or modified to allow for variation and style.
Moonwalk A move where a dancer slides backward while their legs appear to be walking forward.	
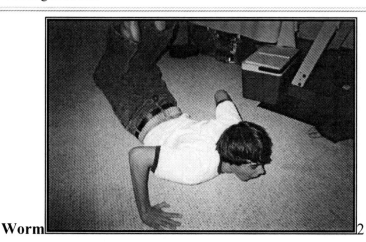**Worm**	A move in which a dancer lies on the ground and forms a rippling motion through his body. This can be done if one of two ways, either forward or backwards, either shifting your weight from the upper body to the lower body (backwards) or vice-versa for forwards.

Break Dancing: Power Moves I

The Windmill

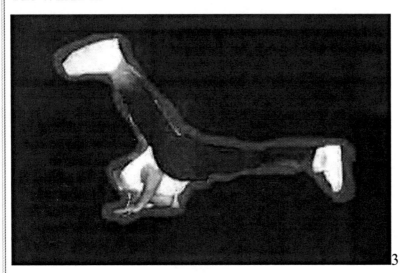

3

Is a move in which the dancer spins from his upper back to his chest while twirling his legs around his body in a V-shape. There are many variations to this move such as nutcrackers and handcuffs. Many dancers will spend anywhere from two to six months learning how to do a basic windmill, since the motion is quite unorthodox.

Headspins

4

The dancer spins on his head, often while wearing a stocking cap or handkerchief. When the dancer uses his hands to aid in speeding up the spin, it is called 'tapping.' A dancer may tap for a few rotations and then 'glide' for as many as 15 rotations. Kid Freeze is the b-boy who claims to have invented the headspin.

Flare

5

Is an incredibly difficult move borrowed from gymnastics and resembles the use of a Pommel Horse, but is performed without one.

Jackhammer

6

Is a move performed on the ground having the dancer balancing on one hand and laying his body on the elbow of the same arm. He then bounces up and down with his hand as he spins around.

Sources:

www.learn-to-breakdance.com/

http://www.colegioamigo.com/alumnos2004/jessica.y.analeyre/pagina3/BREAK%20DANCE.htm

http://www.geocities.com/breakdance_central/graphics/

http://media.collegepublisher.com/media/paper243/stills/147opg43.jpg

www.listentome.net/stuff86.php

www.uic.edu/orgs/kbc/hiphop/break.htm

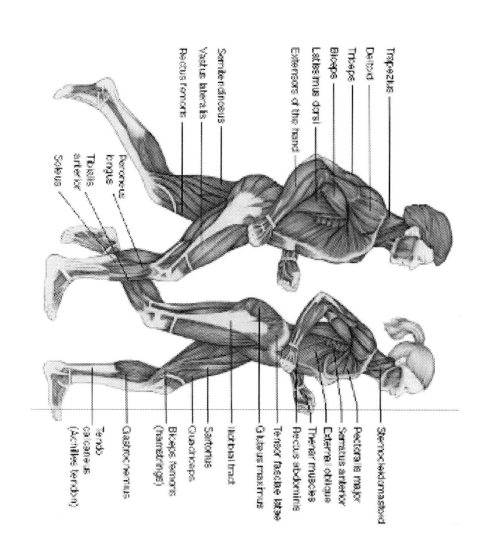

Trapezius
Deltoid
Triceps
Biceps
Latissimus dorsi
Extensors of the hand

Semitendinosus
Vastus lateralis
Rectus femoris

Peroneus
longus
Tibialis
anterior
Soleus

Sternocleidomastoid
Pectoralis major
Serratus anterior
Externa oblique
Rectus abdominis
Thenar muscles
Tensor fasciae latae
Gluteus maximus
Iliotibial tract
Sartorius
Quadriceps
Biceps femoris
(hamstrings)
Quadriceps femoris
Tendo
calcaneus
(Achilles tendon)

149

Song: **"The Science Chant"**   Author(s): Dr. Ron Kelley

It's time for some science yall,

If you listen close, you'll be able to do it all,

In the lab, the first rule is safety,

This is important, so you can make the,

Lab safe for you, lab safe for me,

Can't run in the lab, cause we're accident free,

Now you know safety, the #1 rule,

Now let's get to know a few lab tools,

A thermometer does what, finds temperature,

If you learn the lab, one day, you might find the cure,

For diseases, discover new things for helping,

When a solid turns to liquid, that's melting,

Carnivore, meat eater, herbivore, plant eater,

Gotta know about milliliters and millimeters,

Gotta know the planets, so let's get with 'em,

First we're gonna talk about the inner solar system,

Mercury, Venus, Earth, and Mars,

These are closest to the Sun, we don't wanna be far,

The Sun provides the heat and light we need,

Now here's the outer solar system, yes indeed,

Jupiter, Saturn, Uranus, Neptune and Pluto,

Now let's go back and see what all you know,

If you know the planets, say em after me,

Mercury, Venus, Earth, Mars,

Jupiter, Saturn, Uranus, that's far,

Neptune and Pluto complete the deal,

Now you know the planets, tell me how you feel,

Smart, tell your friends, don't hate,

When water disappears, it evaporates,

Sunlight and water go into a plant,

And oxygen comes back out of the plant,

Sound is cause by vibrations,

Science is done in all nations,

Water boils at 212 degrees Fahrenheit

Water freezes at 32 degrees Fahrenheit,

When water boils, a liquid becomes a gas,

Gravity makes rain drop down fast,

Now you know science, so don't ever say "I can't",

Now it's time to say the Science Chant,

(Chorus)- Science is something I gotta have,

Teacher, Teacher, Teacher, let's go to the lab,

Science is you,

Science is me,

S-C-I-E-N-C-E,

Is so cool,

Is so tight,

Give me a science test, I'll get em all right

Song: "I Can Read More Than You"

Author(s): Dr. Ron Kelley © 2006

Edu-Rap, Volume I CD www.konfidententerprises.com

It's time to talk about the most important skill,

This is the skill, that pays the bills,

The one you need, every minute of the day,

Without this skill, hey yo, there is no way,

To do anything, anything at all,

You need it winter, summer, autumn, spring, and fall,

I'm talking about reading, the #1 thing,

You have to read to rap, and read to sing,

You have to read the plays in football or hoops,

You have to read if you're a part of the military troops,

So get in the habit, read everyday,

The more you read, the more you pay,

Your mind, it's like money in the bank,

Every time you read, you fill up your think tank,

Get your read on, the Dr. K way,

Look at your friends, and I want you to say,

(Chorus)- Yo, I can read more than you,

I can read more than you,

I can read more than you, you, you, and you

Read anything you want, live in the library,

Everywhere you go, a book you should carry,

Now you're gonna have to take reading tests,

So here's some tips, so you can do your best,

The main idea will get you an A,

It's what every paragraph is trying to say,

Compare and contrast, the name of the game,

Check what is different and what is the same,

Who are the characters? What is the title?

What's the story about? this is vital,

That means important, know your vocabulary,

Going a day without reading, now that's scary,

January, February, March, April, May,

Every single month, we read, look at your friends and say,

(Chorus)- Yo, I can read more than you,

I can read more than you,

I can read more than you, you, you, and you

IV. LEADERSHIP AND PEER MEDIATION

> This is one of the most important sections in this collection of lesson plans, because our students are our future leaders, and cultivating their skills should be our top priority as educators.

> A genuine leader is not a searcher for consensus but a molder of consensus.
>
> -Martin Luther King, Jr.

Lesson 1: You Can Quote Me On That!

Using Hip-Hop Lyrics for Critical Thinking

Author(s): Alexander Fruchter

Bio: Alexander Fruchter grew up in Hyde Park on Chicago's Southside. He graduated from Indiana University in 2004 with degrees in psychology and sociology with Highest Distinction. After college, Fruchter joined Teach For America and spent two full years teaching at Henderson Elementary, just a ten-minute drive from his Hyde Park home. After completing his Teach For America commitment, Fruchter was at a crossroads. He wanted to pursue his other dreams of being a writer, obtaining a Ph.D, as well as carving out a music career. However, he was not ready to completely leave the classroom. "You Can Quote Me On That!" curriculum was created and developed in 2006 as a way for Fruchter to remain in the classroom, while also pursuing his other life goals.

Alexander Fruchter is also a well-respected member of the Hip Hop community as a writer, performer, and activist. As the managing editor of SoundSlam.com, Fruchter has written editorials, music reviews, and news stories about Hip Hop culture. He has also conducted over 50 interviews with artists such as Wyclef Jean, the Beastie Boys, Lupe Fiasco, Talib Kweli, Gza, Busta Rhymes, Common, Pee Wee Kirkland, and many, many more.

Grades: 6-8, 9-12   **Subjects:** Leadership, Language Arts, Social Justice

Academic Content Standards: Historical Understanding Standard 2- Understands the historical perspective. Language Arts Standard 4- Gathers and uses information for research purposes. United States History Standard 31- Understands economic, social, and cultural developments in the contemporary United States. Behavioral Studies Standard 2- Understands various meanings of social group, general implications of group membership, and different ways that groups function. Language Arts Standard 8- Demonstrates competence in speaking and listening as tools for learning. Language Arts Standard 2- Demonstrates competence in the stylistic and rhetorical aspects of writing. Music Standard 7- Understands the relationship between music and history and culture.

Overview: Students will learn life skills by reading and analyzing various quotes from individuals involved in Hip Hop culture. Through their exploration of quotes and ideas, they will learn valuable lessons, as well as develop critical thinking skills. Students will also research their favorite quotes and the individuals who said them.

Hip Hop is quickly becoming the most popular form of music, and is considered to be the main voice of America's youth. Therefore the class will be exploring issues such as, the effects of stereotypes, inequalities of education, individual privacy vs. America's safety, and self-confidence/self-knowledge in a language they can understand and relate to, that of Hip Hop. Students will write essays analyzing the viewpoints discussed in class, and questioning the media messages they receive.

Suggested Time Allowance: One Hour

Resources/Materials:

There are no textbooks required to teach this lesson. The reading material will be provided by the teacher will consist of Hip Hop songs, news articles, magazine features, short stories, and interviews.

-Copy of song lyrics (included)

-Student journals

-Pens/pencils

Activities/Procedures:

1. Warm-Up/Do-Now: Why Are We Here?

Quote written on the board prior to class, "My work is personal, I am a working person, I put in work, I work with purpose."—Mos Def

Students discuss what it means to "work with purpose. How does working with a purpose influence success and achievement?"

2. Drugs, Basketball, And Rap

Quote written on the board prior to class, "It's like we're getting caught in a trap, it's the drugs, basketball, and the rap. There's more to us than that."-Talib Kweli

Students will compare and contrast the ideas of multiple authors. Students will use evidence from the text to support their ideas, and respond to the text.

Students will read: "Drugs, Basketball, And Rap"—Talib Kweli (www.ohhla.com)

"Interview With Little Brother" by Alexander Fruchter (attached)

In his song, "Drugs, Basketball, And Rap," Talib Kweli writes that it seems as though African American Youth are caught in a trap of drugs, basketball, and rap, and they are defined by those three fields. In this class students will examine his thoughts by listening to and reading his song. We will then explore the statements Kweli is making, and see how they relate to the real world. We will discuss questions such as:

How do media messages influence the career choices of African American youth as well as other ethnic, racial, and cultural groups?

What societal factors lead to career options being seen as realistic?

What is Talib Kweli's stance on this issue?

Is Talib Kweli's message hurt at all by the fact he is a rapper?

Students may also hear the opinions of Notorious B.I.G., Lupe Fiasco, and Rhymefest, who's latest CD was called *Blue Collar*, based off the concept that you do not need to sell drugs to make a living, or make it as a rap artist. For homework students will read an interview with Pee Wee Kirkland who has started the School of Skills in Harlem, as well as the Hip Hop group Little Brother.

In their interview, Little Brother comment on how media images create stereotypes, and influence the way in which African Americans are perceived by other groups. The group states, "I look at it like, I even posed this question to myself this way, 'yo, if I was an alien on another planet and had never seen black people before in my life, and all I had to go about black people was by turning on BET or MTV or whatever... I'm thinking, they all love strip clubs. They love them. They love chains.... Everybody sells drugs.... That's all they see. So they come to us like, 'Phonte, smoke de chronic? You smoke de chronic?' No, I don't smoke. 'Ahhh, come on. You smoke de chronic. You smoke de chronic.' Naw. And it be making you mad like...But you can't amp on them because they don't know no better. This is all they see. It really just makes you take stock of the music. That's where a lot of the stuff on the album came from. There's nothing wrong with a cat like 50 or Jeezy, or whoever, the street dudes telling their story. But the video outlets and media corporations want you to believe that is the only story and that out of 10, 20, 30 million black people, they speak for the majority. Hell naw. That ain't it. So, that's where that part comes from."

Homework: After the reading students will write about the way in which Hip Hop music both contributes to and also deconstructs various stereotypes. They will begin to questions the media images they see, and reflect on the ways in which those images influence their own thoughts. Furthermore, students will use a stereotype log (included) to document the propagation of stereotypes and the media through which it appears.

Interview: Little Brother's View of Stereotypes In Hip Hop

Phonte: I look at it like, I even posed this question to myself this way, 'yo, if I was an alien on another planet and had never seen black people before in my life, and all I had to go about black people was by turning on BET or MTV or whatever I'm thinking, they all love strip clubs. They love them. They love chains.

Big Pooh: Everybody sells drugs.

Phonte: They all sell drugs. They shoot people a lot. Some of their chains even spin, I don't know what that's about, but they do that. You really have to look at that stuff. We go overseas a lot and it's like WHITE People. It's a different between white Americans and this is WHITE people. The Hitler youth-rally people, blonde hair and blue eyes.

Big Pooh: Their only exposure to black people is what they see on TV.

Phonte: That's all they see. So they come to us like, 'Phonte, smoke de chronic? You smoke de chronic?' No, I don't smoke. 'Ahhh, come on. You smoke de chronic. You smoke de chronic.' Naw. And it be making you mad like. But you can't amp on them because they don't know no better. This is all these people see. It really just makes you take stock of the music. That's where a lot of the stuff on the album came from. There's nothing wrong with a cat like 50 or Jeezy, or whoever, the street dudes telling their story. But the video outlets and media corporations want you to believe that is the only story and that out of 10, 20, 30 million black people, they speak for the majority. Hell naw. That ain't it. So, that's where that part comes from.

Do you agree or disagree with Little Brother? Do you think Hip Hop presents stereotypes that are harmful? Name some examples that you see and hear in the Hip Hop you know to support your opinion.

Drugs, Basketball and Rap **Talib Kweli**

[Talib Kweli]
Yea
S'what I'm talkin about
S-A-S, size ain't shit, neva dat
Strong Arm Steady, Talib Kweli
Yea
[Chorus: Talib Kweli] X2
Niggaz gettin caught in the trap
for the cash, it's the drugs basketball or the rap
there's more to us than that
We the shit consider the facts, afta you analyze that
You know you best to fall back
Woah
[Verse: Talib Kweli]
Woah!
I'm dealin wit, nuttin but facts, when I spit it though
You niggas superstitious don't step on the cracks or split the poem
Candle light, flickers so bright, I feel the wick can kick a sicka flow
and spill it like a liquor store, I spit the shit to make a cripple get up and dance
I spit the shit to make the average MC piss in his pants
I spit the shit to make a mothaf**** call it a night
I spit the shit to see F***wit C Delores Tucker sex like
I take a sip from my creative well, in this game for a minute
I play this well to win it, ya go to Africa like Dave Chappelle, you finished
Cause ya prehistoric raps is borin, the number of whack rappers soarin
like the percentages of teenagers who have abortions
these niggas make they lyrics weak, and they beats is corporate
they try snitchin on records their mouths is leakin ???
drippin em ova system than, Chinese water torture
rippin a series of events, more unfortunate than lemony snicket

CHORUS x2

[Planet Asia]
Yea
medalliance mind, bless the mic for the gods, teach the blind
plus get a piece of mine release ya minds for each design
baby food for thought, rappas not ?? for sport
you ?? pork eatin niggas of sort
yo you's a f***face, burnt out loser that's always up late
planet ais the revolutionary slash nut case
a witchcraft black magic, data load up computers

a spread the message wrote to you where when I show illusions
if all yall niggas is killas then how ya write ya records
how'd you find the time stop lyin ya minds infected
there's only a few, and I ain't sayin niggas don't put it down from you town
I'm talkin bout you
yea the fake dude promotin propaganda, and open on some fanna, and out right snitchin on them cameras
planet ais, gold chain black bandanas low
steady gain click clack rang rang der dey go

CHORUS x2
[Phil Da Agony]
Yea
Just a high skip and a jump
away from gettin everything that I could possibly want
and prostitutes front
get a 4 bar on the roster, scratch that
I'm talkin about a full roster of raps
monstas that rap, buzzed out ?? check the cadence of the frequency
uniquely, we strong arms strategically
easily I twist the ?? killa cali ?? backalleys burnin backwoods in danelis
or
he probably wit Kweli, out in BK
we make it easy for the djs, like instant replays
conversation by the buttons, I talk and touch sumpin
straight shots of the luey he flew me out to London
crunchin numbas flippin more dough, like Cicero
next thing you know we kissin ya hoe, wit out the mistletoe
strong arm steady, agony can ???, Phil da rigglies, the big league niggas is droppin indies
les go
CHORUS x2
[Talib Kweli]
Talib Kweli, right about now
dis what I'm feelin right about now
and I invite you all to check it out wit me
Lets go!

S'like,
X2
niggas gettin caught in the trap
For the cash its the drugs basketball or the rap
there's more to us than that
We da shit consider the facts, afta you analyze that
you know you best to fall back
Woah

Stereotype Log

Directions: Use this log to record the stereotypes you see on TV. Keep the chart with you when you watch TV, listen to music, or are reading a magazine. Fill out the chart to keep track of the stereotypes you see everyday.

Date	Media	Group Stereotyped	Stereotype	Harmful Effects
SAMPLE 10/11/06	*Saved By The Bell TV show*	Women	*Girls are stupid, and obsessed with clothes and fashion.*	Teaches girls that their intelligence is not important, may lead them to not try hard in school.

Lesson 2: Knowledge of Self, Self-Concept

Author: Alexander Fruchter

Bio: Alexander Fruchter grew up in Hyde Park on Chicago's Southside. He graduated from Indiana University in 2004 with degrees in psychology and sociology with Highest Distinction. After college, Fruchter joined Teach For America and spent two full years teaching at Henderson Elementary, just a ten-minute drive from his Hyde Park home. After completing his Teach For America commitment, Fruchter was at a crossroads. He wanted to pursue his other dreams of being a writer, obtaining a Ph.D, as well as carving out a music career. However, he was not ready to completely leave the classroom. "You Can Quote Me On That!" was created and developed in 2006 as a way for Fruchter to remain in the classroom, while also pursuing his other life goals.

Alexander Fruchter is also a well-respected member of the Hip Hop community as a writer, performer, and activist. As the managing editor of SoundSlam.com, Fruchter has written editorials, music reviews, and news stories about Hip Hop culture. He has also conducted over 50 interviews with artists such as Wyclef Jean, the Beastie Boys, Lupe Fiasco, Talib Kweli, Gza, Busta Rhymes, Common, Pee Wee Kirkland, and many, many more.

Grades: 6-8, 9-12   **Subjects**: Leadership, Language Arts, Psychology

Academic Content Standards: Historical Understanding Standard 2- Understands the historical perspective. Language Arts Standard 4- Gathers and uses information for research purposes. United States History Standard 31- Understands economic, social, and cultural developments in the contemporary United States. Behavioral Studies Standard 2- Understands various meanings of social group, general implications of group membership, and different ways that groups function. Language Arts Standard 8- Demonstrates competence in speaking and listening as tools for learning. Language Arts Standard 2- Demonstrates competence in the stylistic and rhetorical aspects of writing. Music Standard 7- Understands the relationship between music and history and culture.

Overview: Students will learn life skills by reading and analyzing various quotes from individuals involved in Hip Hop culture. Through their exploration of quotes and ideas, they will learn valuable lessons, as well as develop critical thinking skills. Students will also research their favorite quotes and the individuals who said them.

Hip Hop is quickly becoming the most popular form of music, and is considered to be the main voice of America's youth. Therefore the class will be exploring issues such as, the effects of stereotypes, inequalities of education, individual privacy vs. America's safety, and self-confidence/self-knowledge in a language they can understand and relate to, that of Hip Hop. Students will write essays analyzing the viewpoints discussed in class, and questioning the media messages they receive.

Suggested Time Allowance: One hour

Resources/Materials:

There are no textbooks required to teach this lesson. The reading material will be provided by the teacher will consist of Hip Hop songs, news articles, magazine features, short stories, and interviews.

-Copies of lyrics for "You Can't Hide, You Can't Run" by Dilated Peoples (1 per student)

-Student journals (1 per student)

-Pens/pencils

-construction paper

-markers, crayons

Quote of the Day written on board prior to class: "They try to box me in, but I got knowledge of self, which is stronger than any cage that you can lock me in."—Talib Kweli

Journal Topic Questions:

-Who is "they" in this quote?

-What does it mean to have knowledge of self?

-How can that help the author break out of the box?

Students answer the questions above in their journals. Students share their responses. Lead a discussion about the quote of the day.

In this quote Talib Kweli is getting out of the box.

*What is the box here?

-Draw a box with a person inside.

*OK, so here we have a box. This box represents the pressures that we may feel, or the ways in which people want to us to act, the things we think we should like to be cool. What are some things that trap you guys in a box? Take suggestions from the class, and put them in the box.

If no one responds you can provide your own examples, such as these:

 *You know what? I'll share a bit myself. I feel that society tells me to dress a certain way, and the way that I dress indicates how people view me. That traps me in a box.

*Sometimes I feel like since I'm a man I need to like action movies, and not dramatic movies, sometimes I don't go to certain movies just because I'm afraid of what my friends might think, and that traps me in the box.

164

*I went to college in Indiana, and Indiana University has a big rivalry with Purdue. We are supposed to really hate Purdue. Sometimes that traps me in a box because I don't really talk to people that went to Purdue.

*I will tell my friends that I grew up on the Southside of Chicago, and they will think that I live in the ghetto and ask me stupid questions all the time. They some times even make me feel ashamed of living here, and I will try to change, and that traps me in a box.

After setting up the box, ask students to help figure out ways in which to get out of the box. Take suggestions from the class.

Pass out the lyrics to "You Can't Hide, You Can't Run" by Dilated Peoples, and play the song for the class (lyrics included).

After students listen to the song ask students the following questions:

*What does the word relevant mean?

*When he says, "the only person I stand in the shadow of is Evidence." What does he mean. How might this help him get out of the box?

*How is the future also history?

*Why does Evidence say that the plot thickens regardless of wealth?

*If you can't run from yourself, what should you do with yourself? (Get To Know Yourself!!!!)

*The Key to getting out of the box is to get to know yourself. Getting to know yourself means developing your own "Self Concept."

-Self-Concept is a social psychology word. I did not learn this until I was a sophomore in college, 19 years old, and you guys are learning it now, so you are way ahead of the game!

If you were you open up a psychology text-book you would get a definition of Self-concept that looks like the following:

"the learned beliefs, attitudes, and opinions one holds to be true about his or her personal existence."

How many people understand this??? We kind of do, we kind of don't, so lets break it down and put it into our own words:

*basically, a self-concept is your beliefs, thoughts, and attitudes about yourself. It is the way you see yourself.

*Self-Concept is the way you see yourself. Your own identity, and how you fit into the world.

*Many people believe that it is the Self-concept that is the biggest motivator of behavior. Watch how this works:

-We all have our own worldview, the way that we see the world (DRAW THE WORLD)

-Then we have our self-concept, the way that we see ourselves in relation to the word (DRAW A PERSON)

-We can see ourselves fitting into the world, not fitting into the world, fitting in a little bit, it is here that we make our box, and we set our boundaries.

*"When people know themselves they can maximize outcomes because they clearly know what they can and can't do."

Your self-concept is not something you are born with. It is something you continually build and change. You form it by doing things, and then thinking about what you have done and how it went. You build a self-concept based on your own expectations and the expectations of others.

There are many self-concepts: physical, academic, social, and transpersonal.

The physical is how we look, what we wear, what we drive, and the possessions we own.

The academic is how well we do at school. It can be general or specific

The social is how we relate to other people

The transpersonal is how we relate to the supernatural.

Now, this is not a college psychology class, so we are not going to spend all our time going over research studies and going deeper into Self-concept. If you are very interested in learning more psychology, please let me know after class and we can talk. What I want to do now is have you guys express yourselves and your own self-concept.

Remember over here I drew myself in the box, and told you some of the things that I feel put me in a box. I'm expected to like action movies, people's view of the suburbs etc…That is the world weighing down on me. Self-concept is my way to get back at the world. And in my box I am going to build my own self-concept, and shape my own reality.

Now, you are going to do this as well.

Students will fold a piece of construction paper into four squares. Each square will be labeled with a self-concept. In each box, students will draw things that describe them and their different self-concepts. Student will then share their work.

Extension: Students will fill out and discuss Self-Fulfilling Prophecy worksheet (included)

"You Can't Hide, You Can't Run" by Dilated Peoples

Any day your last day might come (so)

You can't hide, you can't run

Late night or in the shadows when the daylight comes remember

"You can't hide, you can't run" "Man listen"

Any day your last day might come (so)

You can't hide, you can't run

From the truth, we know each and every day fights come, remember

"You can't hide, you can't run"

[Evidence]

Yeah ("man listen") I stay relevant

Only person I stand in the shadow of is Evidence

Last page, I left off a good look

This ain't the next chapter, it's a whole new book

About to steal the game, I'm a whole new crook

Bakin up that fire, I'm a whole new cook

Get your whole shit took, Cali's back under the sun

So - you can't hide, and you can't run

From the truth, some ain't convinced so they decide to try me

Like I give a F***, we live from India Arie

They got spies in cameras and trailers

We see 'em settin up though we on counter-surveillance

On to me, I'm on to you, it's no mystery

Better think fast though, the future just was history

It's where the plot thickens, regardless of wealth
Cause the worst person to run from is yourself

Self-Fulfilling Prophecy

Directions: Today we learned about the Self-Fulfilling Prophecy.

A Self-Fulfilling Prophecy is a prediction that in being made, actually causes itself to come true.

Read the following scenarios and list ways in which each self-fulfilling prophecy can come true.

1. Jason is going to a birthday party today. Instead of being excited, he is nervous. He doesn't think that anyone will talk to him, and is not looking forward to going. He thinks that most people will think he is boring, and he will spend most of the time just talking to his friend Brandon.

What is the self-fulfilling prophecy?

What are some factors that might make it come true?

2. Patrice has a test on Monday. She is ready, and thinks she is going to do very well. Patrice stayed positive the whole weekend and on Monday she aced her test.

What is the self-fulfilling prophecy?

What are some factors that might make it come true?

Lesson 3: Who Runs The Streets In Your Neighborhood?

Introducing Democracy, The Electoral Process and Government Into The Classroom-- A four-day lesson plan

Author(s): Mark Gonzales

Bio: Mark Gonzales is an HBO Def Poet and founder of the Human Writes Project. He utilizes hip hop culture and spoken word in the classroom to create culturally relevant curriculum that transforms education from a site of social reproduction to invention and imagination. Currently, Mark is pursuing a Masters in Education from the University of California, Los Angeles, and teaching in Watts.

Grades: 9-12   **Subjects**: Civics, Social Studies, American History, Language Arts

Academic Content Standards: Civics Standard 9 - Understands the importance of Americans sharing and supporting certain values, beliefs, and principles of American constitutional democracy. Civics Standard 20 - Understands the roles of political parties, campaigns, elections, and associations and groups in American politics. Civics Standard 27 - Understands how certain character traits enhance citizens' ability to fulfill personal and civic responsibilities. Civics Standard 28 - Understands how participation in civic and political life can help citizens attain individual and public goals. Civics Standard 29 - Understands the importance of political leadership, public service, and a knowledgeable citizenry in American constitutional democracy. Historical Understanding Standard 2- Understands the historical perspective. Language Arts Standard 4 - Gathers and uses information for research purposes. Language Arts Standard 8- Demonstrates competence in speaking and listening as tools for learning. United States History Standard 31- Understands economic, social, and cultural developments in the contemporary United States. Behavioral Studies Standard 2- Understands various meanings of social group, general implications of group membership, and different ways that groups function.

Objectives: 1. Identify Prior Student Knowledge of Government and Democracy 2. List and Define styles of governance 3.Analyze the ideology behind our current notions of democracy 4.Compare and Contrast Government Philosophies and trace the historical context: African, Greek, Romans, and Indigenous tribe 5. Generate knowledge concerning agency: How do youth participate within democracy

Essential Questions:

*Who represents you?

*What does it mean to be a citizen in a society, what does it mean to be a human in humanity?

*Who runs the streets in your neighborhood?

Goal:

*To identify global types of government, contradictions, and alternatives.

*To look at the historical factors that gave rise to our current government and political reality.

*To define democracy and actively ask who participates within a democratic system.

Vocabulary: Word Bank, Government, Direct Democracy, Monarchy, Autocracy, Anarchy, Oligarchy, Human Right, Civil Right, Dictatorship, 3/5 Clause, Citizen, Majority Rule, Consensus, Electoral college

Resources / Materials:

Class Reading Sets: Declaration of Independence:

Frederick Douglas: What to the Slave is your 4th of July

Film/Videos-

Eminem- Mosh (Original & Alternative Endings)

Links: (http://gnn.tv/videos/27/Eminem_s_Mosh & http://www.gnn.tv/videos/video.php?id=28

Audio and Text:

Malcolm X- Ballot or the Bullet

http://www.americanrhetoric.com/speeches/malcolmxballot.htm

Donald Rumsfield: Democracy in Afghanistan

http://www.defenselink.mil/speeches/2004/sp20041004-secdef0801.html

Activities / Procedures:

Day 1: Who Runs Your Streets?

Pre Class Materials and Preparation: Eminem's Mosh Video (Original and Alternative Ending (Available At GNNtv.com) Mosh Lyrics, Butcher Paper, Individual Student Paper and Pencil/Pen.

Write on Board: "Essential Question: Who Runs the Streets in Your Neighborhood".

Intro: (5 Minutes write and 5 Minutes discussion)

Ask students to write for five minutes using the essential question as a writing prompt.

Share answers and write on board. Discussion should be student guided and led, however challenge students to think of ways large gangs/ governments run their neighborhood.

Explain to students the next two weeks will be spent exploring the question, and how it relates to government, money, and our communities.

Group Work (10 Minutes)

Break into groups of five to ten. Ask students to spend the next five minutes listing all the problems that exist in the community. Students are to write down answers on a group list.

The Group List should then be compiled on a piece of butcher paper

(KEEP THIS LIST! it will be used throughout the week.)

Mosh- Video (15 Minutes)

Play Eminim's Video- Mosh (Original Ending)

Explain to students they will be watching a video on government. Ask student to identify what problems are shown in the video (i.e. police violence, evictions, war, racism)? Post- Video students are to identify, compare, and contrast these problems to those in their community; this will be done individually. Then as a group students will share responses and dialogue if they believe the end of the video will solve the problems in the video..

After the dialogue, students will spend five minutes writing an individual reflection on the following topic: *"If you could make your own end to the video, what would you create?"*

Eminem Mosh- Video Alternative Ending (15 Minutes)

Explain to students they will watch the same video with a different ending. Students will be expected to state which ending they feel is more effective, and give one reason why? Students will also share their own ending to the video. This can be done in small or one large group.

End of Class Exercise: S.I.L.T. or S.I.C. (5 Minutes)

Free Write: Something I Learned Today or Something I'm Confused About"

Homework Assignment: This Democracy Called Our Family (5 minute Explanation)

"Government is the way in which people decide the rules and responsibilities of an individual to community. Your family is a government. Tonight, you will interview your parent/ guardian on how they define government and democracy? Ask what are their feelings about the government. After the interview write up a reflection on what government means to you. Think about how problems handled at your own house? Who decides solutions? What about among you and your friends? Minimum of Two Paragraphs Due at Beginning of Class Tomorrow."

Day 2: Our Democracy, Our Definitions

Pre- Class Materials:

Class Set of Word Bank List: With Terms Defined (Found In Unit Outline)

Class Set of Word Bank List: Without Definitions

Class Set of Frederick Douglas's: What to the Slave is your 4th of July (Homework)

Blank Drawing Paper

Write On Board: "Learning Objective: Writing Our World In Our Own Words"

Homework Assignment Report Back/: (15 Minutes)

As students come into the class, assign them into groups of three. Explain to students they will be sharing their homework definitions of Government and Democracy in these groups. Each individual is to share their definition. Together they will come up with one collective definition of the Government and one for Democracy. This will be recorded. After a classroom sharing of collective definitions, students will turn in assignment and definition to the teacher, who will compile onto one document for the following day.

Word Bank and Ethnography: In Our Own Words (30 Minutes)

Explain to students that it is important to not only know conventional definitions to words, but come up with their own, as they just did in the previous exercise and are about to do again. Students will be given the Word Bank Hand Out List with definitions.

Students will spend five minutes pre-reading the list.. Teacher will read a word and ask for a

student volunteer to give the definition, and what he/she thinks that means. After each definition, students will be given a chance to ask for clarification. At the culmination of definitions, teacher will pass out the word bank list without definitions. Students will then write the definition in their own words, as well as a pictoral representation of their definition.

Boondocks Exercise: (15 Minutes) (found at link below)
[http://tradermike.net/movethecrowd/archives/2004/10/the_creative_math_behind_election s.php]

Ask students to share their definition of the Electoral College. Inquire if they have ever heard of the electoral college before today. If so where? Briefly summarize the electoral college, it's creation, and it's role in the 2000 Presidential Elections. Pass out individual handouts, of the Boondocks cartoon as it pertains to the Electoral College. 2 min pre-read, then read out-loud.

Ask students: What does the Boondocks's Huey feel about the Electoral College? Do you agree? Disagree? If you knew nothing about the Electoral College, what are your views now?

Ask students what they think Huey feels about democracy

Do you agree or disagree with his statement in the middle of the second cartoon?

Why would Huey feel this way?

Homework: Today we examined how the world is run in your own words. Huey of the Boondocks is not the first character to criticize the electoral college, voting, or patriotism. Your homework tonight is to read the following excerpt from Frederick Douglas's: "What to the Slave is Your Fourth of July." After reading, draw a picture that either represents Frederick Douglas's view of the 4th of July, your own, or compare and contrast the two. Due tomorrow at the beginning of class.

Day 3: Ballots, Bullets, and Bureaucracy

Pre- Class Materials:

Recording and/or Text of Malcolm X's Speech: Ballot or the Bullet

Recording and/or Text of Rumsfiled's Speech on Partial Democracy in Afghanistan.

Pencil and Highlighter for students.

Scrap Paper

Write on Board: "Learning objective: Does Voting Help Create Change In Your Community?

Intro- (10 Minutes)

173

Students will hand out homework assignment as they enter class. Break Classroom into groups of five. Elect one note taker and one spokesperson. Using the previously created list of community problems (**Day 1 Exercise**), students will decide which problems they think voting will and won't solve. Every student has to vote on a problem and offer one explanation of why.

Post Discussion- (5 Minutes)

Ask the spokesperson from each group to report back on what the majority of their group believed would be changed by voting versus which would not. Spokesperson should give sample reasons from group on why they voted the way they did. The Teacher should keep a classroom tally to illustrate classroom sentiments (tally should be written on the board).

Audio Excerpt: Interactive Text and Music (10 Minutes)

Inform students that they are now going to listen to a speech by a famous Black Activist who fought for the rights of Black People in the 1960's. They are to just listen to his words and guess (theorize) on what he feels about voting.

Play Excerpt Malcolm X's Speech: Ballot or the Bullet- Recommended length: Play from "*When we begin to get in this area, we need new friends, we need new allies.*" through "*No, take Uncle Sam to court, take him before the world.*"...

Ask students what they think Malcolm's attitude about voting. Allow informal conversation, questions, points, or clarifications to be raised. Pass out Text of Excerpt- instruct students they are to listen again and to underline words they don't understand or know, and circle phrases that stick out to them.

Play Excerpt Again (5 minutes)

Socratic Seminar (10-15 Minutes)

After the second play, students can be broken into groups of 5 again, or arranged in a circle to dialogue and share what parts of the speech stood out and why. Inform students that the teacher can ask questions, but this is a chance for them to ask and question one another.

Play- Rumsfield

Listen to Donald Rumsfield Speech on Bringing Democracy to Afghanistan and Iraq

Hand out text of speech.

What does Malcolm feel about voting?

What does Rumsfield express about his views?

What do you feel?

Who do you agree or disagree with? Are there parts of both you like?

Day 4: Where the YOUTH at?

Socratic Seminar

Teacher Preparation:

The Socratic method of teaching is based on Socrates' theory that it is more important to enable students to think for themselves than to merely fill their heads or fish for answers. Socratic Seminar attempt to understand information by creating conversations in class in regards to texts or concepts. In a Socratic Seminar, the teacher removes him/herself from the conversation, allowing students to ask and answer questions of each other. As such the classroom should be set up in a circular, triangular, or square manner enabling students to face one another.

Intro (10 minutes)-

Explain to students that today that similar to yesterday, the will be hosting another Socratic Seminar. However, this time it will be for the length of the class to provide ample time for all voices and opinions to be heard, dialogued, and discussed. Make clear that ideas are to be challenged, but not people. Following is a list of potential questions that can be used throughout the conversation should dialogue slow down. The initial discussion should begin with two questions: Is our government democratic? If so, as youth, how are you allowed to participate in our government?

Potential Questions or Conversation Re-Starters:

As young people, who represents you in government?

When can you vote? When can't you?

If voting is one solution, what are others?

What would you like to vote on?

What are other ways of participating in society besides relying on voting?

Homework: 2 day Assignment

Democracy is founded on the concept of participation. When only part of a community participate, whether willingly or unwillingly, the community is reduced to a partial democracy.

175

Currently, youth are only allowed to vote once they've turned 18, but are required to obey all laws.

Argue whether or not you think youth should be able to vote, or what ways youth participate in democracy, reasons for participating, or not participating, referencing at least two historical documents, three historical characters, and two historical quotes.

This argument can be done in artistic form (i.e. collage, painting, graffiti, a recording, a Play), an essay, or an oral history project (compilations of interviews and recording). The oral history project should include a written transcript of the interview.

Alternative Assignment: Theatrical Conversation with a Historical Figure:

Pretend you are interviewing a person or persons in history about our current reality. What would their opinion be of our system, our leadership, our administration. Write three pages of dialogue where you debate or talk with this person about democracy and government. Include specific references to modern day issues, as well as their historical perspectives.

Possible conversations: Susan B Anthony, Helen Keller, Malcolm X, Patrick Henry, Frederick Douglas, Benjamin Franklin, Socrates, Alexander Hamilton, Madison, Sally Hemmings

Lesson 4: The Game of Life

Author:(s): Andrew Landers

Bio: A. Landers owes unlimited gratitude to his brothers for, among other things, the influence of Hip-Hop on his life. Co-Leader of the Hip-Hop Association's Education Committee, A. holds a Masters Degree in Literacy from The City College of New York and graduated from Boston University's School of Education. Now with five years experience teaching students with special needs in NYC public schools, A. has been an educator since 1995.

Objective: Students will use ideas and inferences from the song "The Game of Life" to make personal and text connections through a discussion and written responses.

Description: After listening to the song and making connections to the novel, Hoops, students will develop critical thinking skills and abstract thoughts to be used in developing a written essay. Target Audience: This activity will be most useful to teachers, students, and youth that are reading the novel Hoops; adaptations can be made to accommodate other situations.

Grades: 6-8, 9-12   **Subjects:** Language Arts

Academic Content Standards: Language Arts Standard 1- Demonstrates competence in the general skills and strategies of the writing process. Language Arts Standard 4- Gathers and uses information for research purposes. Language Arts Standard 7- Demonstrates competence in the general skills and strategies for reading a variety of informational texts. Music Standard 7- Understands the relationship between music and history and culture.

Materials:

Hoops by Walter Dean Meyers , Bantam Doubleday Dell Books, 1981 ISBN # 0-440-93884-8

"The Game of Life (Score)" by dead prez , Soul in the Hole Soundtrack ,Loud Records, 1997

Copy of transcribed lyrics (www.ohhla.com)

Chart paper

Markers

Goals: Students will discuss and write a response to the essential questions, "How is basketball comparable to the 'game of life'?" and "How is Lonnie's life a struggle to win?" Students will also create their own response and definition to the metaphor "life is like a game". In addition, students will write an essay consistent with guidelines previously discussed in class.

Activities / Procedures:

1. Upon completion of the novel, conduct a shared reading session with pages 144-147, and 181-183.

2. Classroom Conversation;

   Discuss the last line of page 147, "You had to live with it until you won, and you could never be sure when you were going to win."

   Discuss Lonnie's quote from page 182, "That ain't the game I'm talking about."

   *In addition to basketball, what could the author be referring to with these statements? How is life like a basketball game? (Chart student responses.)

3. Listen to "The Game of Life (Score)" and ask students to listen for connections to Hoops and Lonnie Jackson's life (no lyrics, just catch the feeling of the song).

4. Listen again using transcribed lyrics.

5. Ask, "What lines from this song are related to Hoops and Lonnie Jackson's life? How do the lines connect?

6. Create a double-sided (T-Chart) with the title "The Game of Life". One column can be titled 'lyrics from Score' and the other 'connections to Hoops'.

   EX. *Lyrics*- "score, this ain't no game this is war". *Book*- Lonnie fought his friends and family trying to get ahead, it wasn't all a casual basketball game.

Evaluation: Students will complete a two-part project. The first part consists of an essay, "How do you think life is like a game?" The essay will follow a previously discussed essay format and will make clear references to the book Hoops, by Walter Dean Meyers, and the song, "The Game of Life (Score)", by dead prez. The second part of the project will be each student's choice. Each will either design a cover for the essay (drawing, picture cut-out, computer graphics) or write his/her own version of "The Game of Life (Score)".

*Covers should contain a visual display as well as the name and title.

*Songs must clearly be original and make references to life as a game and struggle.

Artist: Dead Prez

Album: Soul in the Hole soundtrack

Song: Score

Know what I'm sayin

Life is like a game of basketball

They just want niggas to run jump and shoot

chorus:

The game, of life, is a struggle to survive

We live, to win, cause if we lose, than we die

verse 1:

What's the word for the day homeboy

It ain't nothin but this killin shit

Tryin to get this money right quick

You know how it is

Nigga tryin to eat food and live, smoke weed

Payin rent on my crib so I can breathe

Life is not about the quickest speed

What you achieve

Come to greed by the grief

And what you get is what you see

In your mind visually

And manifest physically

If you stick to it shit'll work out terrifically

Take me, everyday my life be hectic and stressful

Never really know if I'm'a ever be successful

But the best things you get out of life require struggle

If it don't you gettin hustled homeboy

You gettin hustled

How I see it

Anything you wanna be you can be it

If your mind can perceive it

And your heart really believe it

Than you half way there and all you got to do is do it

And if you give it all you got there ain't really

Nothin' to it

Chorus

Score, this ain't no game this is war

Score, this ain't no game this is war

Score, this ain't no game this is war

Score, this ain't no game this is war

(talking in background)

Get your f****** heads in the game, please!

This season don't mean nothin if we lose this!

word up

Verse 2:

As a, black boy

Started out a bundle of joy

but quickly I grew playin with toys

Than you started makin noise as a youth

Tryin to figure out the truth

Behind the shit that the schools ain't tellin

First come rebellin, then come drug sellin

Juvenile court, 'cause you too young to be a felon

Knew that everything around you was yours

But you gotta maintain the game of wealth that the

World has in store

A wise man told you before

You got the power to bring things to life black boy

You can test it

Everything you see is just a thought manifested

But before you had a chance to know that

You got arrested

And it all seems clear to you know, you can breathe

It was different

When you couldn't see the forest from the trees

If you follow your dreams you can accomplish anything

If you always do your best then your destiny is king

Of the world

Chorus

People don't let life, no no

Don't let life mislead you

You have the power

People don't let life

Don't let life deceive you

You have the power

Yeah, score this ain't no game this is war

Score, this ain't no game this is war

Score, this ain't no game this is war

Score, this ain't no game this is war

Verse 3:

Life is like twistin' a blunt, it's how you roll with it

Just figure out what you want and go and get it

anybody tryin' to stop you

For tryin to do for you

That's your enemy dun

The sun be right up in your crew

That's true

Life is a thinking man's game

Use your head for it

Ain't no use in bein' scared a shit

If you prepared for it

Go for what you know good

This whole wide world is your hood

Plus the universe

Cause you was on the planet first

Score, this ain't no game this is war X4

Chorus

People don't let life, no no

Don't let life mislead you

You have the power

People don't let life

Don't let life deceive you

You have the power

Just use your power

Don't be a fool

Don't ever lose your cool

You got the power

V. MEDIA AND TECHNOLOGY

One of the most unique aspects of the Hip-Hop generation (s) is that we are technology savvy. We are also saturated by media images, as are our students. These lessons attempt to deconstruct the media focusing on identity politics and lived experience.

- **Lesson 1: Conducting Effective Internet Research**

  Author(s): Orisanmi Burton

- **Lesson 2: Something You Live—Identity, Perspective and Experience**

  Author(s): Adrian Worrell

In our long, influential tradition, hip hop is the first African-American music that would be impossible without electronic technology. People in our culture have taken turntables, digital samplers, and other dry tech and made them sing....

Hip hop artists took transmitters and turned them into production units, which required a lot of technical mastery. But many people seem to think African Americans are alienated from technology.

I say that the power of hip hop lies in its ability to radically combine sounds, imagery, text, and other media within its form.

Harry Allen Hip-Hop oriented Journalist for over 20 years

wired.com

Lesson 1: Conducting Effective Internet Research

Author(s): Orisanmi Burton

Bio: Orisanmi Burton is a youth worker and organizer at The Brotherhood/Sister Sol. He has developed and facilitated workshops on a variety of topics including human rights, Hip-Hip history, police brutality, and the global AIDS crisis. Additionally, his writing has appeared in The Ave Magazine, Allhiphop.com, and Generation Lion Magazine. He has traveled extensively throughout Africa, Asia, and the Caribbean.

Grades: 9-12   **Subject:** Technology, Language Arts

Academic Content Standards: Technology Standard 3- Understands the relationships among science, technology, society, and the individual. Language Arts Standard 1- Demonstrates competence in the general skills and strategies of the writing process. Language Arts Standard 4- Gathers and uses information for research purposes.

Overview of Lesson Plan: Through discussion, activity and practical research participants with gain a clear understanding of the Internet and the proper way to use it for research.

Suggested Time Allowance: 1.5 Hours

Objectives: Students will:

1. Define and discuss the Internet and many of its uses.

2. Identify and describe many of the pros and cons of exclusively using the Internet for research

3. Discuss the reliability of information obtained from Internet Research.

Resources/Materials:

1. Newsprint

2. Markers

3. A few computers with Internet connections

4. A printer with printer paper.

5. A ball of yarn or string

6. What Is The Internet Handout (attached)

Activities/Procedures:

Defining the Internet:

1. Ask students to call out what comes to mind when they hear the term INTERNET.

2. Write answers on a sheet of newsprint.

3. Once you have a good list on the board see if any of the students would like to take a shot at defining the Internet. (Encourage them to take a risk and not to worry about getting it write or wrong.

4. Read definition of Internet.

   The Internet is a worldwide network of interconnected computers.

Creating a network

1. Explain that this next activity will help to illustrate how the Internet works.

2. Students and facilitator(s) should stand in a circle.

3. Have a student volunteer to go first.

4. The volunteer will start with the ball of yarn in hand and tell the rest of the group 1 thing about themselves that they others do not know.

5. After they tell the fact, they must toss the ball of yarn to another participant in the group making sure to remain holding onto their piece of yarn. NOTE: Participants cannot toss the ball of yarn to the participant directly next to them.

6. Participants will continue this activity until everyone is holding a piece of the yarn and a web is created.

7. Ask the students what we have created with the yarn.

   Explain that this is also how the Internet is set-up. This is what we mean by a network of interconnected computers. The Internet is not located in any ONE place it is spread throughout the world.

Computers that supply data or information are called SEVERS. Those that request information are called CLIENTS. So if you are at home browsing the Internet your computer becomes a client and the website that you are viewing is getting its information from a server which could be located anywhere in the world.

The Internet was created in the 1970s as ARPANET used primarily for military research and communications.

Conducting Internet Research

-Explain that anyone with a little bit of know how can create a website and put their information on the web. There are a variety of different types of websites on the Internet: personal weblogs (blogger.com), commercial websites like (Amazon.com), social networking sites (myspace.com), online encyclopedias (wikipedia) and many more.

-If this is so, how do we know what information on the Internet is reliable?

-The next activity will help us get to the bottom of this question.

1. Break Participants up into small groups so that each group has access to a computer with an Internet connection.

2. Explain to the groups that they now going to conduct Internet research on Hip-Hop. They should approach the research as if they are preparing to write a paper for someone who has no idea about the culture. If they want, they can use the following questions to guide them.

   1. What is Hip-Hop?

   2. What is the history of Hip-Hop?

   3. What are the 4 elements of Hip-Hop?

   4. Who are some notable female MCs?

   5. (facilitator can add more if necessary).

187

3. Participants should print out and be prepared to discuss 4 interesting articles that they find.

4. Students should reconvene and group by group they should share their articles. They shouldn't read the entire article, but sum it up and describe what they think of the article.

5. Facilitator should ask the following questions.

    1. Why did you choose this article?

    2. Do you think the information contained in this article is correct?

    3. Do you think they are from reliable sources? Why or Why not?

    4. Did the website provide citations?

Further Discussion:

1. Distribute the What is the Internet handout

2. Discuss the Pros & Cons of conducting Internet only research.

3. Facilitate an open-ended discussion about the information contained in the handout and the workshop. Academic vs. Non-Academic sources etc.

4. Explain that no matter how you are getting information that the key to good research is to draw from a variety of different sources.

What is the Internet?

The Internet is a series of interconnected computer networks. It was created in the 1970s as ARPANET used primarily for military research and communications.

The Internet is not located in any one place. It is decentralized, meaning It is made up of millions of *SERVERS* located throughout the world. These servers supply the data that users request through a web browser like Internet Explorer or other internet protocols (languages) like FTP or telnet.

Anyone with the resources and a bit of know how can put up a website. All you need is space on a server and a domain name.

So If anyone can have a website, how do you know if the information you are viewing on the Internet is a reliable source?

- How does it look?

  A cheesy looking website can be a good indicator that the information is unreliable

- Does it list sources

Make sure you know where they got their information from.

- What kind of website is it?

There are several types of websites including *Personal Homepages, Blogs, Academic, Commercial, Social Networking,* etc.

Make sure you know what type of site you are viewing. You wouldn't site your best friend's weblog in your research paper for history class.

Make sure you examine multiple sources and compare information.

- Check the (dot) extension.

    - **.com**: is the traditional US extension.

    - **.net**: is a US commerce extension.

    - **.org**: implies that the website is connected to a non-profit

    - **.gov**: is a US Government agency

    - **.co.uk**: is a British extension

Doing a web search via Google isn't always the best option for finding reliable information. *Companies pay search engines like Google and Yahoo to have their website show up first.*

The Deep Web: There are a wealth of academic journals on the Internet which store millions of scholarly articles on a range of subjects from sports to history to nutrition and health. These *full text* Journals (like JStore & Lexus-Nexus) usually require a username password from an institution or college. Most libraries have access to these journals.

Paying attention to any 1 of these tips will **not ensure that the information you are viewing is reliable**. *(At the end of the day, do we ever really know if the info we are receiving is true?).* But keeping all of these tips and tricks in mind and making sure to check multiple sources will help you make the best judgments.

For information on how to properly cite information from the internet see:
http://www.bedfordstmartins.com/online/cite5.html#1

Lesson 2: Something You Live - Identity, Perspective and Experience

Author: Adrian Worrell

Bio: Adrian Worrell has taught in the Greater Toronto Area since 1999. In that time, he has designed courses for students of diverse cultures and learning styles. He currently teaches English and Mathematics at Milliken Mills High School.

Grades: 9-12   **Subjects:** Technology, Language Arts, Social Science

Academic Content Standards: Language Arts Standard 1- Demonstrates competence in the general skills and strategies of the writing process. Language Arts Standard 4- Gathers and uses information for research purposes. Language Arts Standard 7- Demonstrates competence in the general skills and strategies for reading a variety of informational texts. Music Standard 7- Understands the relationship between music and history and culture. Behavioral Studies Standard 2- Understands various meanings of social group, general implications of group membership, and different ways that groups function.

Overview: Seeing something from another point-of-view not only deepens our own experience; but allows us understand others. In this lesson, students learn about the relationship between identity, perspective and experience. Through opinion piece and small group discussion, students will have the opportunity to reflect upon their own perspectives; a short written assignment allows them the opportunity to communicate and expand upon their experience.

Suggested Time: 200 minutes (3 periods)

Objectives:
Students will:
- Work cooperatively in small groups.
- Summarize an editorial piece of writing.
- Engage diverse and sophisticated opinions about Hip-Hop.
- Share their own opinions with their groups and possibly with the class.
- Challenge their own and others' views.
- Write a memoir that details his or her experience of Hip-Hop.

Materials:
- TV-VCR/DVD (optional)
- Video Clip: Brown Sugar – "When I Fell in Love with Hip-Hop" (optional)
- Audio Player
- Song Clips:

  Common – "Act Too" (Explicit Content)

Jill Scott feat. Mos Def –"Love Rain" (Explicit Content)

- Pens
- Paper
- Copies of:
  - Student Handout: "Identity, Perspective and Experience Organizer" (30)
  - Student Handout: "What Does Hip-Hop Mean to You?" (30)
  - Student Handout: "Black Guy, White Music." - Ta-Nehisi Paul Coates (6)
  - Student Handout: "Music Videos Broke My Spirit" - Zulaika Jumarilli (6)
  - Student Handout: "Hip-hop's Disrespect of Women Is Nothing New" - Evelyn McDonnell (6)
  - Student Handout: "Dear Hip-Hop"- Illseed (6)
  - Student Handout: "Tiger Woods Nearly Ruined My Life" – Anonymous (6)

Activities / Procedure:

1. Introduction (15 minutes)

Teacher distributes:

Organizer: Identity, Perspective and Experience

Activity: What Does Hip-Hop Mean To You?

Video Clip (Optional) - Brown Sugar – "When did you fall in Love with Hip-Hop"

Teacher Reads/Paraphrases:

"Several artists used the metaphor of a relationship to describe their experience of Hip-Hop:

the powerful yet conflicted feelings, the hopes, disappointments and opportunities for growth,

make the device a profound one. You might be familiar with these songs:

Audio Clip: Common – "Act Too" (Explicit Content)

Audio Clip: Jill Scott feat. Mos Def –"Love Rain" (Explicit Content)

192

These relationships, like others, are nurturing, wounding and just plain complicated. Our relationships teach us as much about ourselves as it does about another.

Hip-Hop has been described as a culture, as a social movement and as an art form, perhaps it is each of those things, and perhaps it is something altogether different. Nonetheless, it has had immense influence on the world, and on individual experiences.

Hip-Hop's influence goes beyond the way we talk, dress or dance and into what we count and value as "real", how we make sense of the world and who we become. However, each person has his or her own definition and experience of Hip-Hop – and those others experiences and perspectives of others – especially when we disagree with them - are important to our own.

In this lesson you will:

- *Read an article written from a unique perspective.*
- *Work in groups to answer questions*
- *Share your ideas with your peers*
- *Write about your experience of Hip-Hop.*

2. Think-Pair-Share Activity (30 minutes)

Independently, students complete **"What Does Hip-Hop Mean to You?"** They then discuss their responses with a partner and write down their partner's comments and/or questions. The teacher selects students to share their responses. Afterwards, the teacher collects the responses.

3. Jig-Saw: Home Groups (45 Minutes)

Students form groups of five or six (if necessary two students can work on one article). These are their Home groups. Home Group members are named "A", "B", "C", "D", or "E"; and are given the articles correspond with the letters (i.e., A. "Black Guy, White Music", B. "Music Videos Broke My Spirit"; C. "Hip-Hop's Disrespect of Women is Nothing New"; etc.).

4. Expert Group (45 minutes)

Students meet with peers who have the same article (i.e. all of the "A's" together, "B's", "C's" etc). These are their Expert groups. In their Expert Groups, they read the questions, use appropriate strategies to decode the text; write a paragraph to summarize the article; and then collaboratively answer the questions. Note: each student is to have a set of written responses. Teacher circulates to informally assess teamwork and comprehension.

5. Home Group Presentations and Discussion (20 Minutes)

Experts return to their home groups and present their summary and responses. Presentations must be concise; they ought not to exceed 3 minutes. Teacher circulates to informally assess teamwork, comprehension and verbal skills.

Class Discussion (Optional)

For each article, Home Groups identify one quotation that they generally disagree with, one quotation that they agree with and come up with a question to ask the author. These can be used as prompts for the class discussion.

6. Conclusion (15 minutes)

Teacher directs students to **Optical Illusions** and asks student to explain what they see (Answers should vary):
   a) The word "Liar" and a man's face
   b) A vase and the profile of a man and a woman
   c) A man playing the Sax and a woman's face
   d) The face of an elderly woman and the face of young woman (looking away)

Teacher Reads/Paraphrases

If something as simple and straightforward as an image can have so much difference, something as abstract and complicated as Hip-Hop culture is likely to more points of difference and dissention.

Who were are, or at least, who we believe ourselves to be, influences our perspective and how we make sense of the world; and there's more to it. But basically, identity, perspective and experience are interrelated (Refer to Flow Chart Organizer); if you change any one of these things you change each of them.

I like to draw your attention to one of the quotations you looked at today: "Rap is something you do, Hip-Hop is something you live." Hip-Hop is a social movement, a culture and collection of art forms but a common theme is our individuality and subjectivity. To live Hip-Hop means choose the perspective we live in, it means to express ourselves creatively, sometimes competitively. Living Hip-Hop means we can create new names, ideas of ourselves and ways of relating to the world. And perhaps most importantly, through our identity, perspective and of course actions we can control our experience.

7. Evaluation and Assessment

Teacher returns: **"What does Hip-Hop Mean to You?"** and distributes **"Hip-Hop Memoir Assignment"**

Teacher reads through assignment sheet and rubric. Teacher uses the rubric to assess one of the articles (Optional)

Assessment Summary

- Collect student responses to Expert Article
- Observe student participation in small and large groups
- Collect "What Does Hip-Hop Mean to You"
- Collect "Optical Illusions"
- Collect "Identity, Perspective and Experience"

Allow Me to Reintroduce Myself Activity – Identity, Perspective and Experience Organizer

Instructions

- Use the dictionary to define "identity", "perspective" and "experience"; then come up with meaning and example.
- Use arrows, quotations, insights from the lesson or your own opinions to illustrate the relationship between identity, perspective and experience.
- Note: Your organizer will be collected and assessed for effort and completion.

Identity

Definition:

Perspective

Definition:

Experience

Definition:

Allow me to Reintroduce Myself Activity – Perception and Perspective

Name:_____

Tasks

- For each image, describe what you see.
- Write in point form

a)

b)

c)

d)

Allow Me to Reintroduce Myself Activity: What Does Hip-Hop Mean to You?

Name: _____

Tasks

    a) Read each of the quotations below.
    b) Choose three quotations. On a separate sheet of paper, briefly respond to each.
    c) For each quotation use point-form to explain:
        i. Why you chose it.
        ii. Two reasons why someone might reasonably disagree it
        iii. Two reasons why someone might reasonably agree with it.

Quotations

1. "The antisocial lyrics contained in many rap songs and the overall tone of boorish behavior in the hip-hop world is having a destructive influence on many of America's most at-risk children"

    Bill O'Reilly

2. "Rap is something you do, Hip-Hop is something you live."

    KRS-One

3. "Now we know that rap music, and hip-hop style as a whole, has utterly broken through from its ghetto roots to assert a lasting influence on American clothing, magazine publishing, television, language, sexuality, and social policy as well as its obvious presence in records and movies...advertisers, magazines, MTV, fashion companies, beer and soft drink manufacturers, and multimedia conglomerates like Time-Warner have embraced hip-hop as a way to reach not just black young people, but all young people."

    Nelson George

4. "Everybody portrays women in hip-hop as being just interested in ballers, the rollers with the gold."
    Angie Martinez

5. "For many young people - regardless of race, color or economic standing, hip-hop culture is the voice of their often misunderstood and misinterpreted generation - a voice that, up until now, was generally ignored"
    Todd Elliot

6. "Hip-hop is supposed to uplift and create, to educate people on a larger level and to make a change."
Doug E. Fresh

7. "In the hip-hop community, it's about how real are you, or how strong can you be."
Nick Cannon

8. "I grew up around hip-hop so I didn't think it was about being cool or being black or being white or whatever."
Chad Hugo

9. "Hip-hop is definitely not what it used to be, which creative, original music was."
Missy Elliot

10.   "We used to talk about wanting to get some money, but that's when hip-hop was based on your dreams and your fantasy. The whole thing now is the dreams and fantasies were achieved, and you don't want to make it the focal point. You can't keep beating that dead horse."
Sean "P-Diddy" Combs

Allow Me to Reintroduce Myself Reading Activity A - Black Guy, White Music.

Name: _____

Vocabulary	References
Nihilism – the belief that there is no meaning, truth or purpose to life. Surreal – strange or dream-like. Nativist – a point of view characterized by a fear of change. Aesthetic – style or artistic sensibility. Furtive – sly or sneaky.	Rakim – one of the most influential emcees, a pioneer of Hip-hop's "Golden Era" (1988 – 1994). F. Scott Fitzgerald – the author of The Great Gatsby, one of the great 20th century American writers. Led Zeppelin – a famous British Rock group. Soul Train – a television show most popular in the '70's that showcases Afro-American music.

Note: Each group member must have a copy of the responses to share with his or her home-group.

Direct Questions

1. Who were some of Coates' favorite Hip-hop artists?
2. What role did music play in Coates' sense of himself? His identity?
3. What was some of the "white" music that Coates began to listen to?
4. Why was Coates frustrated with Hip-hop?
5. How did listening to "white" music change him?

Indirect Questions

6. How does Coates show the reader that he was a music nerd?
7. What kind of music does Coates listen to now?

Discussion Questions

8. What does your choice of music say about who you are?
9. What were the three most interesting points in this article?
10. Describe the author's relationship to Hip-Hop.

Task – Summary: As a group, use a paragraph to summarize it. Include important details but remember to focus on the main ideas.

Black Guy, White Music.

Ta-Nehisi Paul Coates

In the spring of 2004, I quit hip-hop. It wasn't the first time. Our relationship was stormy from the start. Hip-hop was my first literature, and it was Rakim, not Fitzgerald, who first made me consider writing. Still, all that macho blathering was a weird match for me, a kid with the self-esteem of an earthworm. So every few years, I'd bemoan the state of the music, rip my Public Enemy posters from the wall, unspool all my mix tapes and swear, "Never again!" That was mostly posturing--all it took was something arch and underground, say, Operation Lockdown by Heltah Skeltah, to get me swooning.

But then that spring when I walked into a bar with 50 Cent and Fabolous pumping at maximum volume, it felt like an audio beat down--everything I ever hated about hip-hop blaring at me in all its nihilistic glory. I left with an equally black and dismayed friend. This was absurd--two black men in their late 20s acting like two white women in their early 70s. We could not close the night on that depressing thought, so we headed to another party, where the DJ deftly mixed the White Stripes and Eurhythmics. We sat down. We ordered from the top shelf.

After moving from Delaware to New York City in the summer of 2001, I realized something deep and dear to me was shifting. Despite my stormy relationship with rap, my music collection had always been adorned with a COLORED ONLY sign. But New York's internationalism forced me to rethink my nativist aesthetic. I found myself furtively exploring bands that I would have written off in my youth. Initially I thought this was all temporary and meaningless. But the night I traded 50 Cent for Jack White, I knew something fundamental had changed, that the Soul Train had pulled into its final stop. When I went home that night, it was all devastatingly clear to me. I'd fallen for white music.

As a kid, I had an awful jump shot and no sense of rhythm. I collected comics and played Dungeons & Dragons. I was the opposite of the stereotypical image of a black kid. My most tangible link, the one that repeatedly saved me, was the music. I had all the verses from LL Cool J down cold. In college, I expanded out to Bob Marley and John Coltrane. In short, I was a black-music nerd, for sure out of love but also out of a need to find some common ground with my own. I never explored beyond that, mostly because the kids in my neighborhood believed the words white and music to be antithetical. Occasionally someone like George Michael or 3rd Bass would get a pass. But when we thought of white music, we mostly thought of rock, which is to say loud guitar and long hair.

Then one day I turned 25, turned on BET and realized that the music that marked my identity suddenly had nothing to say to me. I polled my friends and came to the conclusion that I was part of a lost generation--rabid African-American rap fans who had sadly concluded that the soundtrack of their lives was scratched. Most of them self-medicated with Alicia Keys or soft jazz. Others simply turned off the radio completely, preferring to replay the hits of their youth.

I weighed the possibilities, considered the uncharted territory and then began to think the unthinkable. I clutched a copy of Zeppelin II. Was there really something beyond the long hair

and loud guitars? Did all the vague lyrics really add up to anything? Could the last true bastion of cool be hiding beneath a cloak of lame?

I went out with white music like a girl my parents didn't want me to date. I kept the volume low. I hid my new CDs. A new magic poured into me, mostly from Bjork and Yeah Yeah Yeahs. Unlike hip-hop, here was a music that I did not have to reconcile with the fact of being a father, music that had lyrics so surreal that they bent my head into knots. And although my greatest fear still was that a visiting friend would find my copy of Radiohead's The Bends, I was in love again and shocked by what I had to thank for it.

The fact is that white music made me understand how black I really was. I realized that I was connected by experience and history, connected in a way that didn't require recitations of Big Daddy Kane. But more freeing was the simple sense of disconnection--the ability to listen to White Music the way white kids must have listened to jazz, soul or hip-hop. I had no personal stake in the Arcade Fire. I did not have to debate the effects of Foo Fighters on young black youth. For the first time ever, I was just listening to music.

Allow Me to Reintroduce Myself Reading Activity B - Music Videos Broke My Spirit

Name: _____

Vocabulary
Obsession - the domination of one's thoughts or feelings by an idea, image, desire, etc.
Mantra - A commonly repeated word or phrase.
Virility – manly character, vigor, or spirit; masculinity.
Stereotype – a simplified, often prejudicial, image of a group of people.

Note

Each group member must have a copy of the responses to share with his or her home-group.

Direct Questions

1. What made Jumarilli first notice that something was wrong with Hip-hop?
2. Explain three ways that Hip-hop affected her identity.
3. What was the message of "Fatty Girl"? Why did Jumarilli take issue with this?
4. What happened to her social life when she stopped watching videos?

Indirect Questions

5. What role did the music play in Jumarilli's life? Explain.
6. How has school influenced her behavior?

Discussion Questions

7. How are women portrayed in Hip-hop videos? Why do you think this is?
8. Why was Jumarilli obsessed with videos?
9. Describe the author's relationship to Hip-Hop

Task - Summary

As a group, use a paragraph to summarize it. Include important details but remember to focus

on the main ideas.

Music Videos Broke My Spirit

Zulaika Jumarilli

I realized that my music-video obsession had gone too far when I found myself singing along with Snoop Dogg's "Gin & Juice." When the video appeared on BET's Rap City, my younger sisters—Shabi, then 17, and Shaz, 18— and I scrambled for the remote to blast the volume. Bopping along, we sang, "We don't love them hos!" Then I felt sick. I was a junior at Columbia University majoring in African-American studies who ordinarily flinched at the word bitch. So why was it so easy for me to repeat Snoop's off-color mantras? Why didn't I change the channel? Sure, my sisters and I had fun watching the upbeat and sometimes funny videos that accompanied the latest songs without thinking about their implications. But the real answer lies in years of conditioning and uncritical acceptance of television images.

As teenagers and even younger, Shabi, Shaz and I learned to dress, style our hair and speak by watching videos on BET's Rap City or Yo! MTV Raps. When I was 13 and my sisters were only 10 and 11, we dressed up in our mother's high heels and twisted our T-shirts into midriff tanks. Then we danced in front of the TV following instructions from rappers to "Just shake ya rump!" As I got older I bought $20 lip glosses—well beyond my student budget. I even tried to color my hair with Beyoncé's highlights (it didn't quite work out). I dug deep, maxing out two credit cards with purchases for trendy purses and leather boots I could barely walk in.

Then, during my last year at Columbia, something changed. The Ludacris video for "Fatty Girl" was in heavy rotation. The song had sparked a trend validating curvier body images, but I felt conflicted. Rappers seemed to be appreciating a body type that mainstream media would not recognize, but for all the wrong reasons. They only endorsed women's bodies as a focal point in lyrics praising their own masculinity and virility. For the first time I didn't sing along.

After a discussion in class of the complicated history behind Black-female stereotypes perpetuated in the media, my professor pointed out the negative impact of videos on my self-esteem. He suggested I stop watching them for a time to see what would happen. I wondered how I would learn new dances without them.

After two months of video withdrawal, I was bored and frustrated. Conversations with peers dragged when I couldn't discuss the latest artist releases. As I was forced to come up with other topics, my discussions were redirected to current events or our latest reads. When my best friend and I got into a spirited conversation about a book we had both read, we decided to start a book club. Our first title, Finding Fish by Antwone Fisher, was a gripping coming-of-age story. My book-club friends and I related to the main character's struggle with adulthood, sparking animated discussions about our own fears and insecurities. There was much to listen to. I had begun a powerful dialogue with myself and others, and my spirit was expanding. With so much to talk about, I didn't need videos as I once had. My confidence increased as I began to appreciate my own sense of style. I even left home without mascara, and it felt okay.

Sure, I sometimes catch myself falling into old patterns. But I realize that I fall back on my music-video habit when I'm feeling vulnerable. Videos make me nostalgic for a simpler time with my sisters, offering a familiar way to lose myself in the mindless entertainment and forget my problems. I see now that it's better to address whatever's bothering me head-on. Have a good cry. Talk to friends. Exercise. Write. And move on to life's next adventure. Now when I look in the mirror, even when I'm not double-coated with mascara or shimmering with expensive lip gloss, I see a complete person, perfect as I am.

Allow Me to Reintroduce Myself Reading Activity C - Hip-hop's Disrespect of Women Is Nothing New

Name: _____

Vocabulary	References
Drawling – speech that lengthens the vowel sounds	Herb Alpert – Famous musician in the 60's, known for provocative album covers
Modus operandi – the way a person works	
Misogyny – a hatred of women	
Sentiment – a thought or attitude that is based on emotions	
Quandary – a state of uncertainty	
Qualm – a disturbing feeling	
Blatant – a very obvious, purposeful	
Inherent – naturally	

Note: Each group member must have a copy of the responses to share with his or her home-group.

Direct Questions

1. How does McDonell show Hip-hop to be sexist?
2. What are some other sources of sexist images?
3. What conflicts might Hip-hop create in black women or women in general?
4. How has society's response to Hip-hop's offensive lyrics changed?
5. Who does McDonell "blame" for sexist messages in the music? Explain.

Indirect Questions

6. In what ways does Hip-hop affect McDonnell's sense of self?
7. Why do you think McDonnell chose to write about this topic?

Discussion Questions

8. What role do women play in promoting the music's sexism?
9. Why is Hip-hop sexist?
10. Describe the author's relationship to Hip-Hop

Task - Summary

As a group, use a paragraph to summarize it. Include important details but remember to focus on the main ideas.

Hip-Hop's Disrespect of Women Is Nothing New

Evelyn McDonnell

My 12-year-old daughter has excellent taste in music. Ludacris is one of her favorite rappers. She likes one of his hits from his 2001 album Word of Mouf because of its "get outta the way" attitude and drawling hook. When it comes on the radio, it's a great driving anthem, especially in South Florida, where the modus operandi is to act as if you're the only one on the road.

But when I hear "Move Bitch" in clubs, in its unedited album version, it takes on an ominous tone. Then I hear the chorus in full: "Move, bitch! Get outta the way," Bill O'Reilly's favorite pitchman raps. To a female listener, Ludacris' swagger becomes not emboldening, but threatening. "Move Bitch" is another volley in the war of the sexes that keeps turning back the hands of time on an otherwise forward-moving music.

What's a girl to do? You love hip-hop but sometimes you hate hip-hop, because it's hating on you. You idolize the messenger but too often, you have to tune out the message.

Disrespect, if not outright hatred, of women in rap lyrics is so commonplace, it's scarcely worth talking about. The subject lost its punch a decade ago, when conservatives, including some black Democrats, took it up in their all-out attack on the music. For pop's protectors, misogyny became the bathwater; you couldn't throw it out without risking the infant hip-hop. And hip-hop was just too beautiful, bad and vulnerable to risk.

Eminem Trouble

So when an adolescent Eminem wrote "Foolish Pride", an unfinished, never-released, and generally embarrassing track that surfaced recently, he probably thought little of the impact of his rhymes. In the first verses he raps about how important it is for blacks and whites to get along. "When blacks and whites take different sides, unity never happens and we will subside," he clumsily philosophizes. He means, of course, black and white men. Black women are another story, he soon reveals.

"Blacks and whites sometimes mix, but black girls only want your money because they're dumb chicks," Eminem raps. ``So I'ma say like this: Don't date a black girl."

Eminem has apologized for the song. He says he wrote it 15 years ago, long before his recording career and shortly after a bad breakup.

But in "Pride", Eminem wasn't saying anything that many rappers haven't said before or since. The common attitude toward women was long ago summed up by Marshall Mathers' mentor, Dr. Dre: "Bitches ain't s--- but hoes and tricks." That sentiment raised an outcry a decade ago, but nowadays, David Banner casually reaffirms it on his hit "Like a Pimp", and no one says nada. Banner's got some smart things to say about Southern identity, but he's not trying to reclaim the B-word in the way rappers have tried to reclaim the N-word from racists, as a term of pride.

Hip-hop is not inherently sexist. In fact, some of its brightest stars -- Outkast, Missy Elliott, Atmosphere, Mos Def -- infuse their music with love of women. Nor are rappers more likely to objectify and demean women than rockers, teen-pop stars, or Frank Sinatra.

But as in all things, rappers are generally more blatant and unapologetic. Plus, there's a disconnect between hip-hop's pro-black stance and its anti-female tendencies. The music helps black women up with one hand, then shoves them back down with the other. Those women face the same-old feminist quandary: If they criticize their men, they're seen as criticizing their race. And race always comes first.

It was racial, not sexual, lines that Eminem crossed on Foolish Pride. Slim Shady had no qualms about releasing a song about killing his wife, after all, and The Source never asked Eminem to apologize for that track. But the magazine, which unearthed "Pride", seems bent on destroying the rapper's career over it. (The Source has been engaged in a year-long war with Eminem; Pride is merely the ground for the latest, and most public, battle.)

I think there's a more important argument to be made surrounding "Foolish Pride". Why is hip-hop's sexism so casually accepted that a teenage upstart could even write those rhymes? What kind of images of themselves do my daughters see in the songs and videos they love? Do they feel like they have to either bare their curves completely or hide them in baggy clothes? Do they perform psychological gymnastics and distance themselves from hate speech, assuming rappers couldn't possibly be talking about them -- even adopting the misogyny, rationalizing, "Those girls are bitches and hoes?" What does it mean when Kelis, a woman who became famous for her uncontrollable colored afros and burning-bed anthems, poses like a typical Herb Alpert sexpot on her second album? And why is even Elliott standing behind R. Kelly, a man charged with taping sex with a minor? Which bitches, Ludacris, should get out of the way?

Allow Me to Reintroduce Myself Reading Activity D - Dear Hip-Hop

Name: _____

Vocabulary	Reference
Unconditionally – without restriction Notion – opinion, view or belief Rendezvous – a meeting Destiny – predetermined, unchangeable events	"Funky Drummer" – likely the most sampled break in Hip-hop history

Note: Each group member must have a copy of the responses to share with his or her home-group.

Direct Questions
1. Why does Illseed love Hip-hop?
2. How does he defend Hip-hop? How does he explain its problems?
3. Why does he sometimes leave Hip-hop?
4. How does he feel about growth and change?

Indirect Questions

5. What is the tone of the piece? What role does Hip-Hop play in his life?
6. What's the message of the article? Use examples to support your response.

Discussion Questions

7. Under what circumstance might Illseed stop loving Hip-hop?
8. Why do you think that Illseed used a letter to express his thoughts?
9. If Hip-hop wrote back, what would it say?

Task - Summary

As a group, use a paragraph to summarize it. Include important details but remember to focus

on the main ideas.

Dear Hip-Hop

Illseed

I have always let you be you unconditionally. You told me this thing we all had was something new and exciting and liberating. You were free. I feel good about that, that I can accept you totally for what you were, are and will one day be. Totally. That's Love. And that is what I love within you, just you. You too have allowed me to be myself. I'm not one-dimensional. Some days I can be a comedian. Other days a very ugly person. Others still, my heart can flood deep about depression or the loss of loved ones. I can even be happy at times. You love all of me.

It's rare that you can seek and find someone that will accept the complete you with all your flaws and insecurities. We all fall shy of the glory from time to time. And that is the only way I can have this Hip-Hop thing here. Sometimes people would like to have you hate yourself for what you are now, as if you can't change or make mistakes. Or have you hate yourself because you are not what they want you to be. But we all grow and change and change is difficult for people to accept. Growth intimidates people. They cower to it. I gravitate to you, Hip-Hop, because you have grown and continue to do so. People are so quick to dispose of or despise someone because of growth.

Mistakes too. One mistake and people are quick to throw away something that may just need a little nurturing or patience, I have been guilty of this in the past but not with you, Hip-Hop. That will not be the case with you. I have always had a plan for you even though I wanna bail ever so often. Many times you scared me and I thought I was going to lose you because we were going in two different directions, or so I thought. But we were going to the same place. We just took different paths. You just need people - old and young - to relax and work it out internally.

Love. That's not a very popular notion these days, the thought of real love for a person or even an object. Man, people abuse their car the same way they abuse other people. See, real lust is popular these days and love just falls to the wayside. Not with me. If I don't hear from you, I begin to feel anxious and worry as if its not going to hit me up. When I do hear from you, it's like we're back on track like long lost friends. Never skipping a beat, not even a heartbeat or the beat of the funky drummer. The adrenaline rushes through my veins and all my worries are laid to rest. I have a rendezvous with fate and a partner in destiny. Hip-Hop, you are that Destiny. We finally mastered the moment.

Hip-Hop, I'm illseed and you let me in your house when nobody else would.

PEACE! Illseed

Allow Me to Reintroduce Myself Reading Activity E - Tiger Woods Nearly Ruined My Life

Name: _____

Vocabulary
Assumptions – something taken for granted without proof
Cusp – a point that marks the beginning of a change
Poise – a self-confident manner
Frayed – worn away, torn at the edges
Façade – an appearance or illusion of something
Brethren – fellow members, brothers
Elitism – pride in belonging to a favored group.
Affiliated – closely associated
Deception – the act of misleading by false appearance or statement

Note: You may use a scribe, but each group member must have a copy of the responses to share with his or her home-group.

Direct Questions

1. Why did the writer's family admit to having Native Indian (e.g., First Nation) ancestry?
2. How did Tiger Woods affect the writer's identity?
3. What's a "Blasian?"

Indirect Questions

4. Why did the writer keep his background a secret?
5. What role does Hip-hop play?
6. How does the writer poke fun at racial identity?

Discussion Questions

7. Is the writer male or female?
8. How might the writer's secret affect the way he or she related to others?
9. Under what circumstances should someone be deceptive?
10. Describe the author's relationship to Hip-Hop

Task - Summary

As a group, use a paragraph to summarize it. Include important details but remember to focus on the main ideas.

Tiger Woods Nearly Ruined My Life
Anonymous

"You got Indian in your family?"

My big sister has caramel skin and almond-shaped eyes.

"You got Indian in your family, right?"

Her hair is straight and shiny. It reaches the middle of her back.

"You all got Indian in your family?"

"Yes!"

The truth is she just got tired of explaining how a black man from Antigua ended up with a Hong Kong woman. Or why they decided to raise their children in a Philadelphia neighborhood. As for me, I really didn't say much. I was darker, and by 16, I stood 5' 10", had a nice crossover and a jumper that fell like rain. I listened to rap music and most of my friends were black. Behind people's assumptions, my Asian identity faded away. But, in 1997, Eldrick "Tiger" Woods nearly messed that all up.

It had the makings of a perfect American ethnic inspiration story. A young "black" man showed his mastery of a game dominated by old white men. At the Masters tournament, Fuzzy Zoeller, a symbol of the old school, tainted Tiger's triumph with a racist remark. But, Tiger responded with calm and poise, and as he donned the green jacket, African-Americans brimmed with Black pride.

Alas, it was short lived. The bubble burst when he told Oprah and told millions of stunned Americans that he wasn't just African-American, and wasn't just Caucasian or Asian for that matter. He was "Cablinasian", a mix of White, Black, Native Indian and Asian. Looking back now, it seems strange that making himself a symbol of racial unity would piss off so many people. But then again, even I felt betrayed.

After Tiger's declaration, things around my way changed. I caught cold looks and scouring stares from people I'd known for most my life. Hiding my frayed nerves behind a façade of cool, I lived the quiet terror of one who leads a double life. I searched my friends for hints of treachery. I carefully steered conversations away from anything that could expose me as a race faker. I laid low, praying for Venus and Serena to keep winning.

I made it through the Cablinasian crisis fine, I guess. I got more interested in my hidden background. My mother didn't like talking about her past. Despite my knowing a bit of Cantonese, I've been rejected by my Chinese brethren.

Hip-hop wasn't much better.

The music I loved made no mention of Asians unless in mocking and in reppin' the Far East Coast, rap rarely got past Kung Fu flicks, Kanji tattoos and exotic "chinky"- eyed women.

I was under attack from all sides: I felt the racism of those who saw my only blackness and witnessed the racist attitudes of people who didn't know I'm Asian. I was more aware, but I didn't have a sense of who I was. Yet, I knew there had to be others like me. I needed to connect with them. We needed to unite. We needed a label.

I came up with a couple choices and mulled them over for days. "Blackenese" was a favorite, but I figured it'd been taken by a black kid from Japan. "Afro-Asian" was sensible, cool, but a bit too clinical. In honor of Tiger, I settled on "Blasian".

I researched my new identity on the Internet and I was disappointed to learn that I already exist. Blasians were everywhere, in fact we even had our own racial slur: "popolo". But, bigots are nothing if not lazy, they hadn't yet made a ridiculous generalization of us. What's a race without a racial stereotype?

"Given the choice," I typed, "Blasians will pass for a person of a different race, usually black." They sat smugly back in my seat. I had put us on the map.

Next, I decided, we needed heroes, people that Blasians everywhere could feel proud of. Tiger

was a possibility, but I wasn't sure if he was quite Blasian enough. Instead, I settled on Tyson

Beckford, Foxy Brown and Naomi Campbell

I enjoyed about two days of Blasian bliss before I realized that it was all for nothing: when we had another crisis, Blasians wouldn't hold me down, they'd be off somewhere pretending to be Black.

"Well, what else would you expect from Blasians?" I muttered, and blasted up my Wu-Tang CD.

There is talk about rap building a bridge between cultures, being this meeting place of sorts. While that does happen sometimes, not too many people talk about the culture's elitism. Who's in or who's out, who gets respect and who gets clowned has a lot to do with what you look like.

Racism is still very much alive, but things are less tense. Nobody freaks out when Tiger wins yet another tournament or when Jerome Iginla nets the Art Ross trophy. Hip-Hop culture has changed a bit too. DJ Honda and DJ Krush are world famous and work with big name rappers. Kimora Lee Simmons is Hip-hop's first lady and Jin is respected as a great battle emcee.

That being said, around my way, I'm still "black with Indian in my family". And that doesn't bother me at all.

Allow Me to Reintroduce Myself Assignment - My Hip-Hop Memoir

Name:

Marks: __/80

Note

A memoir is much like an autobiography. But in this instance, you won't be writing about your entire life, but describing the ways you have been affected by Hip-Hop culture.

Tasks

- Use the articles as examples and "What Does Hip-Hop Mean to You?" and "Identity, Perspective and Experience" as guides.
- Write a narrative essay (400 to 600 words) use description, events and your unique perspective and identity to tell of your experience of Hip-Hop.
- Include a hand-drawn or digital image that supports part of your memoir.

215

	Achievement Category Criteria	Mark Value	Level Four (80-100%)	Level Three (70-79%)	Level Two (60-69%)	Level One (50-59%)
Hip-Hop Memoir	**Knowledge/ Understanding** Detail and Description	__/10	Cleverly uses detail and description to highlight major themes	Uses detail and description	Makes some use detail and description	Makes minimal use detail and descriptions
	Thinking/ Inquiry Perspective	__/10	Effectively and smoothly engages a variety of perspectives	Considers a variety of perspectives	Considers two perspectives	Considers a single perspective
	Support of Major Idea	__/10	Makes innovative use of reasoning, examples and events	Makes use of reasoning, examples and events	Makes some use of reasoning, examples and events	Makes infrequent use of reasoning, examples and events
	Communication Structure	__/10	Organizes ideas into a highly effective and creative way. Modifies voice and tone to communicate experience	Organizes ideas into a coherent beginning, middle and end.	Organizes ideas into a somewhat coherent beginning, middle and end.	Organizes ideas with limited logic.
	Writing Style and Expression	__/10		Uses a unique voice to communicate experience	Inconsistently uses voice to communicate	Makes limited use of voice
	Application Technical Writing	__/10	Applies grammar, spelling and punctuation rules with a high degree of accuracy and effectiveness	Applies grammar rules, spelling and punctuation rules with considerable accuracy and effectiveness	Applies grammar, spelling and punctuation rules with some accuracy and effectiveness	Applies grammar, spelling and punctuation rules with limited accuracy and effectiveness
	Writing Process	__/10	Rough draft(s) displayed extensive evidence of meaningful revisions	Rough draft(s) displayed evidence of meaningful revision	Rough draft(s) displayed some evidence of meaningful revision	Rough draft(s) displayed limited evidence of meaningful revision

Language Conventions	**Reading and Writing Skills**	**Learning Skills**
☐ Use a variety of sentence types ☐ Pay greater attention to technical aspects. ☐ Refine your use of vocabulary	☐ Pay closer attention to the organization ideas. ☐ Review essay format. ☐ Write with greater clarity.	☐ Make better use of class time ☐ Complete each part of the assignment ☐ Follow instructions more closely ☐ Review notes to clarify concepts.

216

VI. SOCIAL JUSTICE, TOLERANCE AND DIVERSITY

> These lessons are as diverse as their subject matter, attempting to add new elements to the dialogue around multicultural education, complicating it as only Hip-Hop music and culture can.

- **Lesson 1: Prostitution and Sexual Exploitation: Examining Beliefs, Causes, and Solutions to Female Exploitation**

  Author(s): Daniel Zarazua

- **Lesson 2: Ex-Slave Communities in the Western Hemisphere**

  Author(s): Lavie Raven

- **Lesson 3: Me, Myself and I**

  Author(s): Marcella Runell

- **Lesson 4: Instructions on the Effective Use of the Spray-can**

  Author(s): Lavie Raven

The first-ever National Hip-Hop Political Convention took place in 2004 in Newark, New Jersey. It was a four-day gathering, that drew in an estimated 3,000-4,000 was attended by activists, elected officials, political pundits and hip-hop

The dialogue revolved around a variety of topics, including new challenges in electoral politics, rethinking grassroots activism, art and responsibility, and mobilizing the religious community.

Some of the NHHPC's goals include Providing training and organizational support for 1,200 Hip Hop leaders from across the country and Registering over 50,000 young adults to vote

Democracynow.org

2006hiphopconvention.org

218

Lesson 1: Prostitution and Sexual Exploitation

Examining beliefs, causes, and solutions to female exploitation

Author(s): Daniel D. Zarazua,

Bio: Daniel D. Zarazua is currently teaching social studies at Unity High School in Oakland , CA and his teaching experience includes Stanford's Upward Bound Program and the University of Michigan where he received his M.A. in Secondary Education. He's currently serving on the Education Committee of H²Ed, an organization devoted to integrating hip hop into the classroom. Additionally, he's a coordinator for the DJ Project, an arts and entrepreneurial youth program.

Grades: 9-12   **Subjects**: Social Studies, Language Arts, American History, Media Studies

Academic Content Standards: Language Arts Standard 1- Demonstrates competence in the general skills and strategies of the writing process. Language Arts Standard 2- Demonstrates competence in the stylistic and rhetorical aspects of writing. Theatre Standard 6- Understands the context in which theatre, film, television, and electronic media are performed today as well as in the past. Historical Understanding Standard 2- Understands the historical perspective. Language Arts Standard 8- Demonstrates competence in speaking and listening as tools for learning. United States History Standard 31- Understands economic, social, and cultural developments in the contemporary United States. Behavioral Studies Standard 2- Understands various meanings of social group, general implications of group membership, and different ways that groups function.

Overview of Lesson Plan: Through video analysis, discussion, and a reading, students will examine beliefs, causes, and solutions to female exploitation, particularly as related to teenage prostitution.

Suggested Time Allowance: One Hour

Objectives: Students will:

1. Be able to define terms such as prostitution and exploitation

2. Be able to list some of the main reasons that young girls become prostitutes

3. Research and become familiar with organizations devoted to solving this problem

Resources/Materials:

-Copy of "Brenda's Got a Baby" video by Tupac Shakur. Available on several DVDs including *Tupac-Resurrection*

-Lyrics to 'Brenda's Got a Baby," (available online at www.ohhla.com)

-DVD or video player and television

-Pens/pencils

-Notebook paper

-Classroom board

-Chalk or dry-erase board

-Copies of article titled "Law-Enforcement Officials Note Marked Nationwide Increase in Teen Prostitution: Trends" from August 18, 2003 edition of *Newsweek* magazine. Also available online at www.bridges4kids.org/articles/8-03/Newsweek8-18-03

Activities/Procedures:

1. Warm-Up/Do-Now
Write down the following questions on the board: "Why does prostitution exist? What are solutions to prostitution?"

Have students silently write down their responses on sheets of paper. While the students do this, make two columns on the board, one for each question. After a few minutes, ask students to share their thoughts and write down student responses on the board.

2. Show the video "Brenda's Got a Baby."

3. Hand out lyrics to "Brenda's Got a Baby" as a reference sheet and have students silently right down their initial thoughts about the video. While the students do this, make two more columns on the board. After a few minutes, ask students to share their thought about what factors led to Brenda's choices. Write their responses in the first column. Then, ask students what are some of their suggestions on ways that Brenda could have been helped. Write these responses in the second column.

4. Discuss with the students and similarities or differences between the lists of dealing with prostitution in general and with Brenda. Often times, student response to nameless and faceless prostitutes leans more towards punitive measures. The recommendation for Brenda often includes a call for more social services and a stronger family unit. The prostitutes are thought of as criminals while Brenda is seen as a victim. As a result, the discussion can revolve around the need to humanize social issues, such as prostitution, to get a more well-rounded view of the causes and solutions.

On the other hand, some groups of students will generate similar lists for both anonymous prostitutes and Brenda, usually following more on the treatment and service side of things than

220

the criminal side. These pattern can lead to a discussion about why society isn't doing more to combat this issue beyond criminalization.

4. Wrap-Up/Homework: Have students read the articles "Oakland police net 34 in prostitution sting" and "Law-enforcement officials note marked nationwide increase in teen prostitution." These are available at
http://www.findarticles.com/p/articles/mi_qn4176/is_20050604/ai_n15833736

and http://www.bridges4kids.org/articles/8-03/Newsweek8-18-03.html, respectively.

After reading these two articles students should write their thoughts on why young teenage girls are often targeted by pimps. Next students should write why many of these girls get drawn into this type of exploitation.

Further Questions for Discussion:

1. What images in popular media contribute to sexual objectification of women? Note: Bring in

a variety of magazines or other media and have students discuss how women are portrayed.

2. What steps can young people make to combat this issue?

3. What role do males play versus females? Is it different?

4. Why has the word "pimp" used as a positive noun or adjective to describe people and

situations?

Evaluation/Assessment: Students will be evaluated based on participation in discussions, and thoughtful written responses.

Vocabulary: Prostitution, exploitation, gender, abuse, advocacy, juvenile, solicitation, molestation, psychological, esteem

Extension Activities:

1. Students should research how sexual exploitation affects girls and teenagers on a global scale, with a particular focus on why they are forced into this trade.

2. Students should research organizations that deal with stopping sexual exploitation, generating a list of these organizations and the specific type of work that they do.

3. Have students read chapter titled "The Myth of the Great Black Pimp" from Lyrical Swords by Adisa Banjoko and write a response to his critique of pimps.

4. Have students view the Destiny's Child video "Soldier (available on I Tunes)" and read When Will These Sisters Learn?" by Mark Skillz (available online)

5. Students should watch the video and list how men are portrayed and what type of men that Destiny's Child prefers. Then, have students read the Mark Skillz' article and his critique of the

6. Have students watch the music video "Love is Blind" by Eve and write their thoughts on how she deals with her friend's abusive husband.

LESSON 2: Ex-Slave Communities in the Western Hemisphere

Author(s): Lavie Raven

Bio: Lavie Raven is a social studies and language arts teacher of eleven years, who works with students on social justice, community service, and cultural celebration initiatives. Raven has served as a co-founder and as the Minister of Education for the University of Hip-Hop (Healthy Independent People Helping Other People) for the last decade, a multidisciplinary school of the street arts helping youth grow through hip-hop as performers, leaders, and community organizers.

Grades: 9-12   **Subjects:** Geography, World History

Academic Content Standards: Geography Standard 4- Understands the physical and human characteristics of place. Geography Standard 10- Understands the nature and complexity of Earth's cultural mosaics. Geography Standard 13- Understands the forces of cooperation and conflict that shape the divisions of Earth's surface. World History Standard 43- Understands how post-World War II reconstruction occurred, new international power relations took shape, and colonial empires broke up. World History Standard 44- Understands the search for community, stability, and peace in an interdependent world. Historical Understanding Standard 2- Understands the historical perspective. Language Arts Standard 4- Gathers and uses information for research purposes. Theatre Standard 6- Understands the context in which theatre, film, television, and electronic media are performed today as well as in the past.

Objective: Students will learn about two ex-slave communities which thrived for decades in the western hemisphere, and how the hip-hop community can be seen as an artistic ex-slave community.

Time required: 12-14 days

Materials needed: Notebooks, sketchpads, supplies, mural paint supplies, and videos *Quilombo* and *The Matrix*.

Background:

1. The success of slave rebellions and revolts in the western hemisphere has been historically placed in the margins. It is important to recognize that African and Indian slaves did not simply submit to the oppression of slavery, but found ways to resist, rebel, and form their own communities outside of mainstream society. By analyzing the Nat Turner rebellion on the east coast, Palmares in Brazil and the Seminoles in Florida, the importance and success of challenges against slavery can be better appreciated, honored, and celebrated.

2. Palmares was the longest lasting and largest slave community known in the Western hemisphere. This community of ex-slaves lasted almost a century, and grew as large as fifty thousand strong. The capacity to survive in the hills of Brazil against continual efforts of Portuguese slaveholders to destroy the community, is undoubtedly incredible.

The fact that Palmares was also a multicultural community illustrates the ability of a socialist and democratic society's strength under the shadow of a capitalistic slave regime. The arts of breakdance directly descend from such communities, where the dance form *capoeira* was used as a musical martial art against slave masters. The film Quilombo gives a documentary-style retrospective on the long history of the ex-slave community of Palmares.

3. The Seminole Wars were the longest lasting and most expensive wars the U.S. had ever engaged in up to that time. Having forced the Cimarron tribe, also known as Seminoles, into the interior swampland of Florida, the U.S. was never able to extract this community and eventually handed reserve territory over to the tribe. Seminole means runaway, and Cimarron means mixed culture, showing the historical background of that tribe. The Seminoles were a combination of runaway African slaves, indigenous people, and impoverished people from various cultures. The refusal to give up African-American tribal members led to the first and second Seminole Wars.

4. Hip-hop is an artistic rebellion against particular societal restraints endemic to the U.S. The criminalization of hip-hop art forms, and hip-hop's challenges to authority make it illegitimate in society's eyes. Therefore youth shape their own alternative communities where they conspire to create despite issues of private property, private space, and the general repression of creativity. The survival of this community is epitomized in the University of Hip-Hop, a school that stresses the cultural survival of its art forms and practitioners.

5. *The Matrix* is a film that presents an ex-slave community struggling to survive in an imagined future society. In this society computers and technology have overtaken humanity, and actually control human actions. These technological forces thrive on the consumption of human bodies and program human minds to believe in a false and safer rendition of reality. Those with the greatest ability to challenge the technological repression are computer hackers, who have penetrated the network, and are fighting to reveal it to all humanity. A group of rebels has discovered this subterfuge, and are struggling to break down the submission of human to technological forces.

Additional Sources: *Children of God's Fire* by Robert Edgar Conrad, *Lies My Teacher Told Me* by James Loewen, and the film *Stony Island*.

Getting Ready:

1. Instructor will give historical background on Palmares and the Seminole Wars in the form of articles, book excerpts and documentary pictures from the times.

2. Students will form a definition of slavery, and delineate differences between physical and mental slavery, and discuss how both act in combination.

3. Students will review the historical role of slavery in different societies (i.e. indigenous people of the Northwest coast, the internal African slave trade, Chinese slavery, and the

enslavement of women in many societies), and its contributions and detriments to localized society and the worldwide community.

4. Students will write a pre-conceptualizing essay, where they will state their feelings and opinions on slavery.

5. Students will prepare their drawing materials for sketching perceptions of ex-slave communities, their inhabitants, their architecture, and their defense systems.

Activities / Procedure:

1. Students will view the film *Quilombo*, taking note of the musical score, the social commentary, the dance routines, and the character development. After viewing the film students will reflect on their own previous knowledge of such communities, and address the importance of Palmares to the historical record of liberation efforts of all oppressed people.

2. Breaking into groups of 3-4, and using art supplies, sketchbooks, and notebooks, students will design their imagined version of how Palmares was situated geographically. Students will outline and discuss the social organization structure and societal beliefs within Palmares. An architectural student from ITT can help in these designs.

3. Students will read over the history of the Seminole Wars and using a map of the United States, draw a path showing the forced migration of indigenous peoples from Oklahoma to Florida.

4. Students will compare the geographic location of the Seminole communities and Palmares, and discuss the need for inaccessibility to these communities. Students will also speculate on the ready defense networks used against entreating governmental forces.

5. Students will go the library and identify a list of possible foodstuffs, local fauna, climate, and geography available where these ex-slave communities would have grown. Students will discuss the role of *self-sufficiency* and interaction with the environment in maintaining these communities for such long periods of time.

6. Students will discuss the different types of slave resistance, as outlined by Noam Chomsky: *resistance, rebellions,* and *revolts.*

7. After viewing the film *The Matrix*, students will evaluate the various ex-slave communities they have studied, comparing and contrasting the motives and accomplishments of these rebellions and revolts.

8. Students will design and paint a mural depicting the historical importance of ex-slave communities, bringing their studies to a visual form which can be shared with the Chicago community.

9. Students will discuss aspects of hip-hop history and its art-forms which could explain its role as an 'ex-slave' arts community; does hip-hop qualify as a revolt, a rebellion, or as a resistance movement?

10. Students will identify other subcultures that could qualify as `ex-slave' (or Maroon) communities.

Assessment:

1. Students will discuss their ideas from the first essay, and write a second at the end of the unit, which will address how their perspectives have expanded regarding slavery and resistance against it.

2. Students will present their community designs to the group, and discuss the strengths and weaknesses of their designs, and how aspects of all the groups' designs could possibly be combined.

3. Students will submit one page of written reflection on each film.

4. Students will be expected to bring back four examples (pictures, drawings, written descriptions) of the natural environment surrounding one ex-slave community of their choice.

5. Students will document the execution of the mural with video, photographs, and audio recordings; following the completion of the mural, students will give an oral presentation and explanation of the mural to other SWYC youth.

6. Students will each circulate and submit three petition sheets for the Anti-slavery movement, as they relate to challenging present day slavery.

Lesson 3: Me, Myself and I

Author(s): Marcella Runell

Bio: Marcella Runell is a doctoral candidate in the Social Justice Education Program at University of Massachusetts, Amherst. She has been an educator for over ten years, currently serving as the Education fellow for the Tanenbaum Center for Interreligious Understanding. In addition, Marcella is a freelance writer for the New York Times Learning Network and VIBE magazine, an adjunct faculty member for the Bank Street College of Education and Co-Director of the H^{2}Ed initiative.

Grades: 6-8, 9-12   **Subjects:** Civics, Fine Arts, Language Arts

Academic Content Standards: Civics Standard 9 - Understands the importance of Americans sharing and supporting certain values, beliefs, and principles of American constitutional democracy. Language Arts Standard 1- Demonstrates competence in the general skills and strategies of the writing process. Language Arts Standard 2- Demonstrates competence in the stylistic and rhetorical aspects of writing. Language Arts Standard 8- Uses listening and speaking strategies for different purposes. Behavioral Studies Standard 1- Understands that group and cultural influences contribute to human development, identity, and behavior.
Behavioral Studies Standard 2- Understands various meanings of social group, general implications of group membership, and different ways that groups function. Visual Arts Standard 3- Knows a range of subject matter, symbols, and potential ideas in the visual arts.

Overview of Lesson Plan: In this lesson, students will focus on cultivating symbols of their individual identities, and write college admissions essays based on various identity exercises.

Time Allowance: One Hour

Materials:

-pens/pencils
-classroom board

-copies of college essay guidelines

-materials to create and hang sketches of symbols of identity (color pencils, paper, markers, tape)

Objectives: Students will:

1. Evaluate the unique and common identities of their classmates by participating in "Step Into the Circle."

2. Assess their own level of identity and symbolism by creating a word web, T-group, and identity symbol and sharing the results with the class.

3. Synthesize the results by creating an actual college admissions essay based on their identity symbol and its significance.

Activities / Procedures:

1.WARM-UP/DO-NOW: Students will participate in an activity entitled "Step Into the Circle: or cipher. Students will form a large circle (cipher) where everyone who is able is standing in the outer circle. Teacher will read a series of statements and if it is true for the student, they are instructed to step into the circle. For example, "Everyone wearing sneakers, step into the circle." Students will notice who is in the circle, and who is not, and then return to the outer circle. The purpose of the activity is to see where students share common ground, as well as uniqueness in their identity and experience. Teacher should call the first few statements to set the tone, and then if appropriate students can create their own statements. Typically students should be instructed to call statements that they can identify for themselves, rather than "out " other students.

Suggested statements (from lower risk to higher risk; encourage students to come up with their own statements as well.)
Step into the Circle if the following statement is true for you:

1) You listen to Hip-Hop.
2) You ate breakfast this morning.
3) It took you longer than a half hour to get to school today.
4) English if your first language.
5) You know at least five of the elements of Hip-Hop culture.
6) You have mixed ancestry.
7) You practice a religion other than Christianity.
8) You have a Myspace page.
9) You have traveled outside of the United States.
10) You are a member of a sports team.

Teachers and/or students should feel free to create their own which may be based on television shows, movie preferences, music tastes, extracurricular affiliations, diversity in families or geography, social identities such as race, class, gender, ability, religion, or sexual orientation.

After students have completed the activity, they should have a discussion using the following questions.
-What did you notice about yourself during the activity?
-What did you notice about other people during the activity?
-Did you learn anything new about this group?
-How did it feel to participate in an activity like this?
-Do you think this activity is representative of your school? Why or why not?

-Do you think diversity is valued at your school? Why or why not?

-What does it mean to be an individual within the context of a larger community?

2. Expanding on the first activity students will begin to think about their identity by creating a poem that is a word web. They will write their name, and then add adjectives, nouns, verbs or adverbs that describe who they are. After they have completed the word web, students will create a t-chart of their own personal strengths and weaknesses. They should include at least three for each side. The t-chart will simply be the letter T drawn with strengths in one column, and weaknesses in the other column.

After they have worked on developing their strengths and weaknesses, they should begin thinking about who they are and what symbolizes their identity. Do they have a particular symbol that they identify with? If so, what is it and how does it reflect them? Or, would they like to have a symbol that reflects who they are. What would it be and why? Ask students to sketch the symbol and then post them around the room.

Explain to students that they are going to be crafting a college essay for homework that is based on who they are and why they have chosen the symbol. Students will explain to the class why they have chosen their symbol. Students should have a chance to present, discuss and ask questions as a class what the different symbols mean to the people who created them. Questions for follow up may include: "How well do you think your school encourages you to be yourselves? How well does the larger society honor and encourage you to be yourself? Why do you hold that perspective?"

Students should be given guidelines for creating a 500-word college essay that is based on the common application essay which allows students a topic of their choice as part of the admission process (http://commonapp.org/#).

Guidelines might include (and can be copied on a hand-out for easier access):
-The topic is describing what is unique about yourself based on your word web and t-chart, as well as your symbol. How might you turn this into a question to guide your essay?
-What might your main point or thesis be for the essay?
-How might you craft an outline for the progression of your essay?
-Will your essay be chronological/sequential or a different format?
-What type of opening first paragraph will you create? Will you lead with a quote or anecdote?
-Have you thought about your paragraphs and topic sentences? If so how will they work to transition your thoughts?
-How will you provide support for your statements? Will you use examples from your life experience?
-How will you conclude the essay? Will you refer back to the opening paragraph or will you reiterate a general theme from the essay?

3. WRAP-UP/HOMEWORK: Students will craft a 500-word college admissions essay on themselves and their unique identities. The essay is based on the activities in class.

Further Questions:

-What does it mean to identify yourself in relation to others?

-What are some of the benefits of being in school with people who are different from you?

-What are some of the benefits of being in school with people who are similar to you?

-What other societal symbols of identity are you familiar with?

-Do members of your community have symbols of identity that you are familiar with? If so, what are some examples?

-How important is music to your personal identity? What cultures do you identify as being a part of?

Evaluation: Students will be evaluated based on participation in the initial activity, creation of identity symbols, and successfully crafting a college admissions essay.

Vocabulary: reinterpreting, accurately, subversive, distinctive, donned, serape, intervene, obscenities, obligation, escalated

Extensions:

1. Using all available materials, create a collage of photos, magazine ads, or other materials about what it means to have a contemporary adolescent American identity.

2. Craft a poem in any style you choose entitled and themed, "What It Means to Be Me."

3. Create an illustrated Life Map, which uses a timeline of key moments of your life from birth to now. Examples include moving, new siblings, changing schools, religious celebrations, monumental family occasions, etc. Your map should be illustrated, using words, sentences, or symbols. It can be linear and chronological or open-ended.

Interdisciplinary Connections:

Media Studies-The film "Mean Girls" depicts clicks in high school, and stresses the importance of identity. Write a review comparing it to the social structure in your school.

Teaching with The Times-Scan The Times for all articles that are focused on teenagers especially in regards to identity. Create an annotated bibliography of them for other students in your class. Post it on a bulletin board to educate members of your classroom community.

Lesson 4: Instructions on the Effective Use of the Spray-Can

Author(s): Lavie Raven

Bio: Lavie Raven is a social studies and language arts teacher of eleven years, who works with students on social justice, community service, and cultural celebration initiatives. Raven has served as a co-founder and as the Minister of Education for the University of Hip-Hop (Healthy Independent People Helping Other People) for the last decade, a multidisciplinary school of the street arts helping youth grow through hip-hop as performers, leaders, and community organizers.

Grades: 6-8, 9-12   **Subjects**: Fine Arts, Social Justice, Physical Fitness

Language Arts Standard 1- Demonstrates competence in the general skills and strategies of the writing process. Language Arts Standard 2- Demonstrates competence in the stylistic and rhetorical aspects of writing. Language Arts Standard 8- Uses listening and speaking strategies for different purposes. Behavioral Studies Standard 1- Understands that group and cultural influences contribute to human development, identity, and behavior. Behavioral Studies Standard 2- Understands various meanings of social group, general implications of group membership, and different ways that groups function. Visual Arts Standard 3- Knows a range of subject matter, symbols, and potential ideas in the visual arts. Physical Education Standard 5-Understands the social and personal responsibility associated with participation in physical activity.

Overview:

The techniques used here specifically extend from the Spray Brigade School of painting, where ways of painting have been passed down from Zorro, Rafa, and Jecko, of the original Ice Pack crew. These techniques can be used with youth or artists of all ages, to build their bodies (shoulders, arms, forearms, wrists, hands, and fingers) up for painting. The exercises are suggested to all writers as a way of maintaining the body's painting abilities, and of keeping the essential painting body actively engaged in physical and kinesthetic activities related to spray-can use.

UHipHop/Prograniecze program in Sejny, Poland (2003)

Suggested Time Allowance: One hour

Objectives:

OVERSTANDINGS ABOUT SPRAY-PAINTING

Students will learn that:

1. The spray-can is itself a body. It is a container of paint mixed with propellant, whereby a straw carries the paint from the can out of the cap or nozzle, and onto the wall.

2. As a body, the spray-can breathes. The air and paint come out of the spray-can's mouth, and a writer can HEAR the way that a can breathes. With the proper control of the finger and directional painting, one can know the abilities of a writer by LISTENING to their can control techniques. Does the can breathe right? Is it struggling? Is it forced? Is it smooth like butter?

3. One must learn how to use the entire body for painting. The painting stance has often been compared with fencing. The body must be able to bend low, reach high, and make adjustments, all, within the frame of its physical ability to do so. A painter has a strike box of sorts, which dictates the range that your body can reach from its original position. Reaching beyond that strike box can make painting difficult, so know your range of movement and keep your body flexible.

232

4. Repetition is necessary for improvement. At the beginning a writer needs to hone his/her can control skills. Once you have the ability to control a can (physical technique), you can further your style (mental technique) by continually experimenting with coloring, letter formation, and new ideas. It is always important to challenge oneself to move beyond what you know best. It is when you surprise yourself, that you make the leaps and bounds as a writer. Without practice, there can be no growth or evolution. The mind and body must work together to become better at painting. As you improve your physical technique and embrace stylistic challenges, eventually you will become one with the spray-can, and your spiritual relationship with writing graffiti will take you to places that you have never been before.

5. There are no mistakes in spray-painting. Have no fears. Anything can be repaired, and if you're a real warrior there will be many more days of painting.

Resources/Materials:

-spray paint cans

-bricks

-canvas or open area

-copy of questions for analysis

Activities/Procedures:

1. Warm-Up/Do-Now:

GETTING READY- PHYSICAL EXERCISES

Form a circle (a cypher) with all of the writers. The exercise will be done facing one another. Be sure to count all exercises aloud together so that the power can be felt in the cypher.

Warm up the body: Begin by jogging and/or doing a set of 25-50 jumping jacks to get the body warmed up.

Warm up the arms: Do 21 full circle turns with your arms, as though you are swimming. Stretch your arms as much as possible while doing turns. Do the turns in both directions. Then, do a set of 21 shoulder rolls, to the front and the back. After completing these exercises, shake your shoulders up and down to get the blood flowing.

Warm up your hands: Begin by clapping your hands together slowly…then speed up the clapping…speed it up…then slow down the pace of the clapping until there is none. Proceed to rub your hands together, to get the blood flowing in your hands. This step is very important because this how you bring your bodies heat and potent energy to the hands. You will feel the warmth in your hands when you are doing this warm-up: this is the necessary energy that flows out of your body, through your hands, into the spray-can.

2. Shake all cans: Everyone should come together to shake the cans. Then everyone will be given a brick, or a full can for the exercises. It is preferable to have an object heavier than a spray-can, so that the hand is over-challenged. Then when the spray-can is in your hand, it will be lightweight and easy to manipulate. You will use these bricks for the following exercises.

Each of the following exercises emulates motions that writer must make for certain spray-painting movements. All students must be sure that their can faces straight ahead, that your fingers are on the nozzle, and that you don't allow the can to stray from a forward painting angle. You must imagine that you are at a train-yard or at a wall painting. Do not rush through the exercises. The stroke technique used here is not speedy, but paced to the actual speed the paint is propelled from the can. Post up in a stance where your legs are about as wide a party as your shoulders, and your knees are slightly bent.

Horizontal Lines: First, identify your strike box. Do not reach beyond your opposite shoulder when doing this exercise. Hold the can at chest level, and proceed to carry you arm across, as though you are painting a straight horizontal line. Do not press the nozzle. This is only an exercise. Proceed to do strokes from left-to-right. Each stroke must pause at its beginning and end. Do 21 strokes in that direction. Then, do 21 strokes from right-to-left. Switch the brick to the other hand, and do the same exercises with the other hand.

Vertical lines: Again, identify your strike box. You will now do imaginary lines from your forehead to your waist, down the center of your body. Do 21 repetitions. Then, do your strokes in the opposite direction, from your waist to your forehead. Switch the brick to the other hand, and do the same exercises with the other hand.

Circles: Holding the brick at face level, you will paint an imaginary circle that goes as low as your belly button. Begin by doing the motions clockwise. Do 21 repetitions. Post the can at the top of the circle, and go ahead and do 21 reps counterclockwise. Switch the brick to the other hand, and do the same exercises with the other hand.

Diagonals: Hold the brick at shoulder height. You will now paint imaginary diagonal lines from the upper-right corner of your body, to the opposing lower left corner of your body, at about waist height. Proceed to do 21 repetitions. Then, take the brick and paint imaginary lines in the opposite direction. This exercise requires you to bend you knees more than the others, and be sure to aim your can straight at your imaginary surface.

Warm-down: Put your bricks at your feet. Do another set of jumping jacks and repeat the hand warm-up listed above. Your hands and arm are now ready and warmed to begin painting.

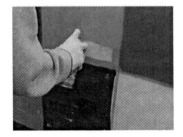  

University of Chicago Graffiti class (Spring 2005)

IMPORTANT PAINTING TIPS: START/STOP TECHNIQUE

- When teaching students how to paint, we use the Spray Brigade start/stop technique. This technique requires discipline, and once a writer has mastered the technique, he/she can move into other ways of doing strokes. The most important thing here is the STROKE. Every line that you do is a practice line for your final outline. In this manner the can is completely familiar to your body by the time you have to do the best fine art work on you piece. With this technique, you start to paint a stroke, and when you are done, you stop painting. A line has its beginning and end. DO NOT OVERLAP STROKES. Your goal is to paint lines better and better each time. Even for those just beginning, you will see dramatic results in your painting abilities if you apply the start/stop strokes. This technique also distinguishes messy writers from clean writers. You will be forced to learn how to do straight lines, perfect circles, and clean outlines.

- This technique is best taught within a fixed painting space. Outline off a space (a square) and you fill in this square by doing the inner outline of the shape first, and then fill in the space with the start/stop stroke technique. This technique can be used to build basic

235

backgrounds for beginning writers. Instructors should set up backgrounds or pieces that students can fill-in, thus learning clean painting within a limited space.

- After several specific practice runs (really several days or hours of continual practice), students should be given their own space to work with, where they have to apply the start-stop technique.

Muslim Youth Center mural by Raven and youth (Summer 2005)

4. **Wrap-Up/Homework:** Students should choose a piece of graffiti to analyze in their local community. They should answer the following questions (copied on a hand-out for easier access):

1) What is the location of the piece you have chosen?

2) What does the piece say?

3) What are the colors of the fill-in?

4) What are the colors of the 3D?

5) What is the color of the outline?

6) What is the color of the aura or glow?

7) What are the colors of the background?

8) Describe how colors are used in the piece.

9) What do you think of the piece you have chosen?

10) What is the message or theme it is trying to get across?

Additional Hip-Hop Education Resources

Compiled by Marcella Runell

www.H2ed.net

Hip Hop Education 101 article for VIBE (overview of Hip-Hop education as a "movement"). http://www.vibe.com/news/online_exclusives/2006/09/hip_hop_education_101/

Lesson Plans/Curriculum:

Words, Beats and Life Hip-Hop Journal:
http://www.wblinc.org/journal/issue1/poetry/women.html

Hip-Hop Science CD can be found-http://www.emusic.com/label/115/115844.html

Hip-Hop as an Educational Literacy Program (H.E.L.P.) has comprehensive lesson plans for teaching language arts/literacy skills for 13-18year olds,http://www.guerillaartsink.com/

The **Rappin' Mathematician** is a great resource with accompanying CD's at www.mathraps.com.

Ron Clark from the recent TNT movie, has a CD, which teaches the presidents, the bones of the body, and other interesting and useful lessons including knowledge about MLK, Jr., and South Africa. www.ronclark.com

The **New York Times** provides FREE interdisciplinary lessons for educators teaching grades 6-8, 9-12, with at least fifteen specifically using Hip-Hop, http://query.nytimes.com/gst/learning.html?lquery=hip-hop&grade=6-8%2C+9-12

The **Rock and Roll Hall of Fame** has a comprehensive list of FREE interdisciplinary lesson plans created by fellow educators on various genres of music for various grade levels, including Hip-Hop at http://www.rockhall.com/programs/plans.asp.

Flocabulary is an amazing resource, and they have a new book coming out Winter 2006 on Hip-Hop History, as well as several FREE lesson plans accessible on their Web site, http://www.flocabulary.com/teacher/lessonplanmosdef.html.

The Hip-Hop Circuit: Teachers hiphopcircuit.com/teachersup.htm
A tremendous resource for using hip-hop in education. FREE lesson plans, articles, unit materials.

Hip-Hop Poetry and the Classics for the Classroom
hiphopintheclass.com
Alan Sitomer and Mike Cirelli co-wrote an instructional guide for how to incorporate hip-hop

into the classroom specifically through language arts skills. At this site, teachers can see some sample lessons and order the book for more information.

Flipping the Script: Critical Thinking in a Hip-Hop World
http://www.justthink.org/flippingthescript/ A curriculum for teaching students media literacy and other topics using hip-hop music and culture.

VH1 has FREE curriculum to accompany their Hip-Hop programming **And You Don't Stop: 30 Years of Hip-Hop**, which can be found at http://www.vh1.com/partners/vh1_music_studio/supplies/specials/downloads/hip_hop2-lesson5.pdf#search=%22hip-hop%20lesson%20plans%22.

Yale-New Haven Teacher's Institute provided a nice three-part lesson on Graffiti at http://www.yale.edu/ynhti/curriculum/units/1993/4/93.04.04.x.html.

Ithaca College hosts a Web site called, **WISE (Working to Improve Schools and Education)** which has FREE lesson plans, articles, and other useful resources on Hip-Hop and education, http://www.ithaca.edu/wise/topics/hip_hop.htm

PBS has a FREE lesson plan on Transcending Jazz, Poetry and Hip-Hop, which can be found at, http://www.pbs.org/jazz/classroom/transcend.htm.

The **United Human Rights** Handbook Web site offers ten FREE lesson plans, at http://www.unitedmusicvideo.org/html/lessonplan.html, which utilize some Hip-Hop.

Lesson Planet costs money, but you can get a free seven day trial for what seem to be some interesting lesson plans that focus on hip-hop and dance at http://www.lessonplanet.com/search/Art_and_Music/Dance?startval=10#.

Organizations:

Hip-Hop Matters, Executive Director Andrew Ryan, hosts a Web site (www.hiphopmatters.org) with educational resources as well as information on *The Journal of Hip-Hop*, which provides a space for critical dialogue about hip hop culture (http://www.johh.org).

The **University of Hip Hop** Web site (http://uhiphop.uchicago.edu) provides a useful model for educators seeking to implement hip hop education programs

The **Temple of Hip Hop**, founded by KRS-ONE, has a mission to promote, preserve, and protect hip-hop as a strategy toward health, love, awareness, and wealth (www.templeofhiphop.org).

Russell Simmons, in partnership with the Urban League, created a literacy program for NYC high school students called **Hip-Hop Reader** (http://www.nyul.org/whatsnew.asp?intCategoryID=75&intArticleID=442)

Kanye West, also has a innovative education program called, **Loop Dreams**, http://www.erniebarnes.com/kanyewestfoundation.html.

Recent Films:

Byron Hurt's award-winning film "Beyond Beats and Rhymes: A Hip-Hop Head Weighs in on Manhood in Hip-Hop Culture" (2006) is available with a teacher's guide (http://www.bhurt.com)

Award-winning documentary on Hip Hop and education, "Reading Between the Rhymes," (2005) by filmmaker Keith Morikawa. (http://www.uthtv.com/about/team/)

Dead Prez (www.bossupbu.com) has a Web site that offers relevant educational information on various topics for the community, also check out the Starz in Black documentary on Bay Area Politics, "It's Bigger Than Hip Hop."

Useful Web sites:

Daniel Zarazua, Oakland based DJ/Teacher hosts a Web site (www.domingoyu.com) with up-to-date information on education and identity.

The mission of the **Hip Hop Archive Portal** housed at Stanford University is in part to facilitate and encourage the pursuit of knowledge by creating a resource guide of: hip hop-related books, articles, and courses (www.hiphoparchive.org).

Hip-Hop Congress, http://www.hiphopcongress.com.

National Hip-Hop Convention http://www.2006hiphopconvention.com/

Davey D http://www.daveyd.com/

Children's Books:

Author Nicole Duncan-Smith's new children's book *I Am Hip-Hop* http://www.allhiphop.com/hiphopnews/?ID=6271

Hip-Hop Kidz http://www.h2kz.com/ (*Bring it On* and *Bust a Move*) books

Bust a Move #2 (Hip-Hop Kidz) by Jasmine Beller (Sep 7, 2006)

The Cheetah Girls series (Deborah Gregory)

Brook, Sally. *Hip and Hop.* London: Blackie Childrens, 1987. Illustrated.

Parker, Vic. *Bearobics: a hip-hop counting story*, New York: Viking, 1997.

Vozar, David. *M.C. Turtle and the hip hop hare: a happenin' rap.* New York: Doubleday Dell,

1997.

Wade, Gini. *Curtis the hip-hop cat*. London: Macmillan Children's, 1986.

Campbell, Mary. *Hip hop happy!: adventures in physical activity for 3-5 year olds*. Ottawa: Serious Fun Enterprises, 1994.

Dargaville, Michael. *The hip hop leap frog: a novel*. Bungendore, N.S.W.: Central Sun Books, 1995. Illustrated.

Body Parts Rap 4 Kids: An Activity Book 4 Hip-Hop Kids, A Leader's Guide 4 Parents, Teachers, and Friends of Children by P. Thandi Hicks Harper (Jan 10, 2005)

How to Draw Hip Hop by Elizabeth Bush

I See the Rhythm http://www.childrensbookpress.org/community/rhythm.html

Gangsta Coloring Book http://www.ayejay.com/books.htm

Hip Hop Land by Omar Shaheed (April 1, 1997)

Hip, Hip, Hooray Day!: A Hip & Hop Story by Barney Saltzberg (April, 2002)

BRATZ! Sasha: Hip-Hop Hot! (Bratz) by Nancy E. Krulik (Jul 28, 2003)

Shanna's First Readers Level 1: Hip, Hop, Hooray! (Shanna's First Readers) by Jean Marzollo (May, 2004)

From the artists:

Common *I Like You, But I Love Me, ME: Mixed Emotions ,The Mirror in Me, Hug Me, It's Okay*

Queen Latifah *Queen of the Scene* book and CD

Doug E. Fresh *Think Again* book and CD

LL Cool J *And the Winner Is* book and CD

Will Smith, Kadir Nelson (Illustrator) *Just the Two of Us*

Hip Hop Immortals: The Remix by Bonz Malone, Nichole Beattie, and DJ Lindy (September 2003)